Irene Dish ♡

9/4/06

To my very dear friend
Irene.

Sylvia Rauzi McElroy

2-22-07

Walk Brave
Walk Strong

JOSEPH RAUZI

Sylvia Rauzi McElroy

Paisa Publishing Company
De Pere, Wisconsin

Photo on page 146 courtesy of Lee Barber.

Cover design: Douglas Hjorth

Additional copies of this book are available for
$15.95 from:

Sylvia Rauzi McElroy
2680 South Van Buren St.
Green Bay, WI 54301-2914

Printed in the United States of America

Library of Congress Control Number 2006902374

ISBN 0-9764782-3-4
Published by Paisa Publishing Company

Dedication

In gratitude to my parents, Joseph and Pauline Rauzi
and
to my husband, Tom, and our children
Monica, Tom, Denise, Joseph, David, Kathleen
and their families.

CONTENTS

Joseph Rauzi

A young Alpine boy journeyed with inner strength and physical strength through ninety-two years of life. A life filled with events each a fascinating story in itself. Stories ranging from childhood adversity to obtaining rights for his fellow workers; from snubbing Mussolini to a possible movie career; from train robbery to rescuing people from the trouble in their lives; from standing unafraid against the Mafia to working till the age of eighty-nine. His life. Joseph, a common laborer, husband, father, an upright man.

ACKNOWLEDGMENTS

When reading books, I often wondered at the way an author would go on and on giving acknowledgments and thank-yous to people who assisted in the writing of the book. Now that I have written this book about my extraordinary father, I understand their undying gratitude toward those who helped, encouraged, and challenged them in their writing.

Having said that, I would like to say that even before my father died, I knew I had to write this story but I lacked a professional writer's education. When I wrote the first chapters, I greatly doubted my ability. I gave those chapters to my friend and avid reader, Father Jim Quinlan, who responded with valuable suggestions, and then he said, "It's a good read, Sylvia." Those words often carried me through when self-doubt raised its troublesome head.

A couple of chapters later, I asked yet another friend to read them, Helen Benton, an English Literature adjunct professor. She also enjoyed reading the chapters, so I continued. To both Helen and Father Jim I extend my gratitude. They were the light on my path. Much later, Helen read through the finished manuscript for me, making needed corrections and helpful suggestions. She also edited my rewrite. Helen doesn't realize how much I depended on her and how much I admired the very gracious manner in which she willingly worked on my behalf.

Then there was my friend, Bobbie Charneski, who I teasingly named "thorn in my side," because she would read the chapters I finished and say, "But, Sylvia, I need more information and the readers will question, too." She always was asking for details on events, people and situations. I was also reluctant to write about difficult personal things and she made me see that it was necessary to do so. She caused me to think more clearly and accurately. Papa's story is richer in content because she urged me to be more complete in my telling of it. I am so grateful for the honesty and trust of her friendship which enabled her to urge me on to better writing.

Many thanks also to my friends, Barb Loritz; Bishop Robert Morneau; Barb's son-in-law, Doctor David Spika (whom I never met). They all read Papa's finished story so that I could have their opinion of its merit, giving me their comments, which I needed to hear.

I want to thank Deborah Hufford of Sundance Creative Services, who so willingly gave me her time and knowledgeable advice on the necessary requirements in approaching publishers to hopefully interest them in my book.

Thank you to our daughter Denise, who lifted a concern off my mind by carefully copying precious old photos of Papa and family for me.

Thank you to my friend and grade school classmate, Mary Jo Hank, of A&M Secretarial Services, who enthusiastically did the final preparation of my manuscript, making it format-ready for submission to publishers.

Finally,my heartfelt gratitude to my publishers, James,Audrey and Pamela Alt, for their advice, insights, encouragement and much needed support --all of which has brought me to the completion of this marvellous journey through Papa's life which I can now present to you, the readers.

To all these wonderful people, I extend my gratitude and hope that they know how much I value their input and their generous willingness to help.

PROLOGUE

The year before he died, my father and I sat over a period of days with a tape recorder sitting on the diningroom table between us. I asked him to tell me about his life. At first he was nervous and fidgeted with the tape recorder. You can hear a lot of tapping and crackling sounds at the beginning of the tape. Then he relaxed and forgot about the recorder as he remembered and told me story after story, answering most of my questions. Just a few were things he didn't want to say; some of the information I already knew through the oft-repeated accounts of his life and my observations over the years.

Occasionally in the tape you hear my mom's voice in the background as she offers some correction of facts or suggestions of information. Not too many years later she lost her memory and unfortunately I was never wise enough to sit at the diningroom table with her with a tape recorder between us.

I'm Joseph's sixth child of seven children. When just old enough to understand, I began listening to his stories – what imaginative wonder they held for me!

Up to my late teens I saw Papa as a hard-working and good man. He was honest and holy, strong-willed but with patient endurance, a lover of stories and humor, and the owner of a fascinating history. Everyone I knew respected him and I was so proud he was my father. That his job was not prestigious was of no consequence to me. He was a cemetery laborer and later a janitor.

In my adult years Papa and I were very close in a quiet way.

We enjoyed so many things in common, especially a good story, a funny joke, and a good actor on TV. Before I got married we went to Mass together every morning.

During the last two decades of his life, we no longer seemed to need words. He read my face, I read his. We often knew each other's thoughts. Unspoken communication was commonplace. On the last day of his life our eyes spoke volumes and we were at peace together with his dying.

In these pages I give him to you. You'll enjoy him. He will echo your own life's pain and hopefully empower you as you read of his victories. I know you'll enjoy his stories.

At times I will quote his words as he spoke them in his Italian broken English so that you can taste the flavor of his personality and deep feelings. Let's begin ....

O, wonder!
How many goodly creatures are there here!
How beauteous mankind is! O brave new world,
That hath such people in't!

(Shakespeare)

CHAPTER 1

BIRTHPLACE AND EARLY YEARS

Papa was the fourth of nine children of Archangelo and Maria (Flor) Rauzi. They were farmers who reflected the image of their small Austrian town, an image of poverty and dignity. Archangelo was highly respected for his integrity and as an outspoken leader in community affairs. This very fact would be the reason for the humiliation which Papa endured at the age of fourteen. I will tell you that story later. Throughout his life, to his ninety-second year, he would tell that story with such sadness. His body would slump and his voice would be unsteady at times. At the end, he would straighten himself, squaring his shoulders, lifting his head, and he would say, "I never forgot it."

The earliest records of Papa's family in Cloz, Austria, is of the marriage of Pietro and Angela Rauzi in 1601. Joseph was born at the turn of the century, July 20, 1899, in Val de Non, Cloz, Trento, Austria. It was a small community of approximately sixteen hundred people; farmers, craftsmen, carpenters, one cheese maker, one miller, and a few merchants.

Cloz is located on the side of a mountain in the Alps. At the time of Papa's birth this Trentino area was part of Austria. After the First World War it was annexed by Italy. Its history is ancient, and it was a stronghold of the Roman Empire because of its location. Roman political enemies were also exiled to this wilderness area. The castles they built still remain, high on Alpine cliffs. Wealthy Roman exiled people and also those still connected to Rome nestled themselves safely against the sides

of the mountains or at the highest elevations to protect themselves from invaders. Some of these castles are still inhabited.

Embedded in an embankment along the main road in Cloz is a sealed glass case which contains artifacts. During recent road repair Roman artifacts were found as the workmen were digging. Earlier in the 20th century a famous serpentine arm bracelet belonging to a documented Roman woman known as the Giantess (because of her tall stature) was found by my mother's grandparents as they were digging on their property. The jeweler told them it was junk jewelry and gave them ten lire for it. Six months later, while on a vacation, they saw the bracelet in a museum in a glass security case.

In this town of ancient history, Joseph's birthplace, the homes were mostly built as row houses; very large, two- or three-story homes, built hundreds of years ago. Ceilings in the homes were high, curved, vaulted Gothic ceilings. Ancient frescos adorned the outside of many homes. Farmers lived in a cluster in town but their fields were up the slopes of the mountain. Most of the homes had animal shelters below on the first level and living quarters on the top levels. Large rounded arched doors on the first level allowed animals, carts, wagons and farm equipment to enter.

A common sight on the farm homes are large rounded, arched doors.

Balconies, with flowers flowing over and cascading down their beams, face the majestic Alps and valleys below, echoing the beauty of the multicolored flowers which grow wild on the slopes. Up in the rocky area of the mountains, above the vegetation line, only the hardy, furry Edelweiss grows out of the cracks on the side of the mountains. Small towns are scattered in the sweeping valley below, between the mountains.

This was a place of natural beauty, where poverty was worn with dignity. When I asked Papa why he left such a beautiful

Beautiful flowers adorn the houses in the small towns in the Alps.

place, he replied in a tone revealing loving memory but not regret, "It was beautiful for sure, but the living was poor."

The town had one main stone and dirt road on which barefoot children toughened their feet. Numerous roadside shrines, lovingly built, stood as holy sentinels as the inhabitants of Cloz, whose main mode of transportation was walking, passed by. The road came up one side of town on an incline and down the other side on a slight angle. Almost at the center of the road stood one of the two ancient churches, Saint Stephan's. A walkway around the church was mosaic, fashioned from colored stones, one of the remnants of old art and a tangible reminder of Roman ancestry.

Art used many forms of its language in speaking to Cloz of its ancestry; the architecture of the churches, also chapels and castles high in the rugged mountains; sculpture, mosaics and frescos inside and outside of churches and homes, painted centuries ago and still remaining without being renovated; building structures, reliefs, wood carvings, brass and copper pottery and decorations; poetry, music, songs, and story-telling. An amazing richness of human creativity.

Papa gave an interesting insight about that main road through town and Saint Stephan's. He said that the people from the left branch of the road always sat on the left side of the church, and the people from the right branch of the road always sat on the right side of the church. He never knew why; they just did. The townspeople gathered not just for Mass at Saint Stephan's but also for Vesper prayers and the blessing of Benediction in the late afternoon.

There is a small cemetery along the main road of town. It is enclosed by an eight-foot masonry and stone wall. At one end facing the road is a large wrought iron gate and, at the opposite end, facing the valley and the mountains, stands a small chapel. Each family in the town has a plot where all the members of the family are buried. These plots have cement enclosures approximately a foot high. Inside the enclosures families plant flowers.

There are also large headstones and statuary such as Papa's family plot which is of granite and black marble with a white carved angel approximately five feet tall standing on a granite pedestal in front of it. Once a month, but not in the winter, people from Cloz gather in the cemetery and stand by their family plot as a Catholic Mass is

The Catholic cemetery in Cloz, where memorial Masses are held in memory of loved ones.

celebrated in memory of deceased loved ones on an altar which has been set up outside the chapel on the landing of the steps.

When I visited Cloz for the first time in July 2002, I was fortunate to be able to stand with my European cousins by our family plot for one of these Masses. Before leaving the cemetery I took a little dirt, stone, and a tiny pinecone from the ground inside the plot and brought them home to the United States. There was a respectful silence during this event. People came in quietly and took their places near their family's grave. All the men took their hats off. Enthusiastic visiting started only as they left through the gate after Mass.

There is another beautiful custom in Cloz that my father talked about. One of my cousins sent me a tape cassette recording of it. On Sundays, each of the churches in each of the little towns scattered in the mountains and its valley in the area which is called Val de Non, ring their church bells at a specific time – one following the other and then together. The bells echo, ricocheting from mountain to mountain. What a soul-stirring sound.

The church itself, as in all small farm communities, was the center of social life. Papa said, "There was one Victrola and a guy who played the accordion in our town – that's all. No radio, no telephone, no nothing." Young men would put on plays at the church during winter months for the entertainment of the whole town. Papa added, "There were no automobiles to get around, either; just two guys who owned bikes, the jeweler and another guy who owned the store. They would bike five miles to the next town, Fondo, if there was an emergency and some medicine or help was needed."

Besides Saint Stephan's Church and all the activities going on there, there was a smaller church, also built centuries ago, Santa Maria's (Saint Mary's), its interior walls covered with faded but still beautiful frescos. This was not used as a parish church at the time my father lived in Cloz, but rather as a chapel. Men from Cloz who had become priests and were serving in other towns and countries would say their Mass at Santa Maria's when visiting home.

Because of the love and pride of their history, the townspeople kept this small church of past centuries maintained and open. Papa said they did this through legacies left in their wills. Today, the small, intimate Santa Maria's is where daily Mass is celebrated. Sunday Mass is said in the large Saint Stephan's Church.

Some of the priests followed their immigrant countrymen from Cloz to new countries. They went as missionaries, in the hope of giving their people stability of faith in new countries and cultures. Immigrants, likewise, would settle in towns where their local men were now missionary priests.

Saint Stephan's and Saint Mary's, located just a short distance from each other along the main road, were the anchor of this little town of Cloz, as they had been for centuries, with the people, their homes and farm fields nestled all around them.

Off the main road were many side streets with homes in rows and clusters and a central water fountain within these clusters. Women gathered around the fountains to rinse out their clothes, which they first hand-scrubbed in tubs at home with water heated on their stoves. They also visited, as neighbors do, while doing their wash. Ice cold water in these fountains came from constant streams of water flowing down the mountain. The sound of water rushing can be heard underfoot and at open streams in various areas of town. During my visit in 2002, I took a picture of a man washing his clothes at the fountain near my grandparents' home.

Papa's family home, as well as all the others in town, were built of hand-hewn lumber from the surrounding Alpine mountain forests, and also of stones, mortar, stucco and hand-crafted

A man washes his clothes at a fountain in Cloz, just as his parents and ancestors did many years ago.

copper. Most of the centuries-old homes had walls of rock and mortar that were more than a foot-and-a-half thick. This was to ensure structural stability and to act as an insulation against the cold and heat. These homes were the places where many of the townspeople lived and died, never having left their valley.

The Rauzi home was the last home at the end of their road. They lived on both the ground level and second floor. Even though they had a barn separate from their home, the home still had the large, arched double doors. In the past there had been a stable. It also was an advantage being the last house on the road because they were able to have their barn close to them instead of some distance away. It was just across the road from the house. Interestingly, the ceilings in their barn, built of stone and mortar, had the rounded Gothic ceilings just like the home and public buildings. The entrance to the barn sloped downward from a higher elevation.

Across from the barn was another road, with one of their fields opposite. Farmers bought little pieces of land scattered here and there, up the slopes, as they could afford them. Papa's family grew the produce they needed for the year: potatoes, corn to grind meal for polenta, flax, hay for a few head of cattle, grapes for wine, apples and other fruit to eat, and vegetables for the table. The land was rocky and poor. Factory-produced fertilizer was not yet invented, so crops were not always good. They were resigned to this fact and, as Papa said, "What came up, came up." Eventually, apples became a major product with their specialty being a very excellent Golden Delicious apple.

Those who had some cattle spread whatever manure they could collect onto their fields. Papa lugged buckets of manure to the fields with the help of his younger sister, Gelinda. She would push as he pulled and lifted the bucket up the slanted entrance of the barn. Papa's great-grandparents bartered with the owners of the barn for permanent use of the barn. The Rauzi family still uses it.

When not busy with farm chores or school, most of the family's living in Papa's home took place in the kitchen and in his parents' bedroom, called "la stua" (which means family room in our Italian dialect). Except for the wooden floor in the parents' bedroom, all the floors in their home were of a poured, smooth substance, but not cement, my father said. He could not identify what it was.

An oblong, dark wooden table dominated the kitchen, the top of which had to be refinished by Archangelo from time to time to erase the wear and tear caused by a family of eleven. Little children sat on a long bench on one side of the table, while unmatched chairs were used on the other three sides. An open cupboard held the necessary dishes.

Pots and pans hung from hooks on the wall. Both the windows and the rounded archway of the front entrance door were set deep into the thick walls. The kitchen's light came through them and a single light bulb at the end of an electric cord which hung without a lampshade from the ceiling. Papa said, "I remember, but barely remember, when the electric first came in." The ceilings in the kitchen, like the rest of the rooms, were rounded Gothic ceilings. Water was carried in from the outdoor fountain in the piazza which flowed continuously near their home.

An iron wood-burning stove was used to heat the kitchen and for cooking. A series of graduated size rings could be removed from the cooking surface so that the bottoms of heavy, hand-crafted copper kettles could be set down into them. Venting from the stove went into a ceramic wall behind it. This ceramic held the heat and radiated it. Heat from this stove was also vented into the parents' bedroom. Behind that ceramic wall was a small unlit corridor, dark and warm, where Papa's mother, Maria, breast-fed her babies in modest privacy.

Except for the parents' bedroom, where the babies also slept, the bedrooms were unheated and ice would form on the inside of the windows in winter. The family gathered in the parents' room around a long wooden table to do their homework, sewing, and other needlework or projects. Sick children were nursed in the parents' large bed, and a cradle stood near the bed all the years the children were being born. Approximately six-foot-high raised wood panels covered the bedroom walls in two contrasting wood finishes. A lovely needle-worked linen made by my grandmother hung on a wooden rod on the wall for decoration. In later years, two large studio portraits of my grandparents, in ornate, dark frames also hung on the walls along with religious pictures and a crucifix.

The Rauzi family was middle-class in the social strata of Cloz – not the poorest, not the richest. Their meals were plain, unvaried, with almost no delicacies. Babies were breast-fed. When old enough, children drank chicory coffee with some milk in it, like everyone else. "We never drink the milk because we sell it for making cheese and butter. The main product of the family," Papa explained. "No, no, there was no milk. They never give the children a glass of milk or a bottle." Real coffee was reserved for illness, important visitors, or grand celebrations like a First Communion. It was carefully stored away for such occasions. Papa also said that despite the fact that they had four cows they seldom saw meat on their table.

Breakfast was always patate rostede (pan-fried potatoes), and most often leftover polenta (solid corn meal mush) chopped up and fried together with some onions. The day's soup was started early in the morning, cooked in a copper kettle. It was a barley vegetable soup called menestra. Soup, polenta and cheese were eaten at noon. For supper, the left-over soup was thickened with corn meal and extended with water or a little milk and fat so there would be enough for everyone.

There would also be potatoes, sauerkraut and a little salad at the evening meal. Fruit would be their dessert. At Easter and Christmas they had what Papa called, "the big meal." It was pasta. When I asked him what was used to flavor the pasta, his ninety-one-year-old eyes twinkled with savoring delight as he said, "Butter and anchovies, the nice little salty things, was cut up and tasting good."

I asked Papa why they never ate bread. "Bread? Well, we had home bread. You can buy it, too, but we never buy it because it was costing money. We make rye bread but not too often because it cost money for the flour. We had no much money."

"Didn't you ever have sweet things, Papa?" I asked. "Huh, sweets? We never see no sweets." He went on to say that when they made their First Communion, his mother would put a white tablecloth on the table and they would all have real coffee and bread for breakfast instead of chicory coffee and patate rostede. A visit to an unmarried aunt's home that day or on their birthday would be the only time he remembered eating sweets. She would make them a sugared tortella, which is like a pancake.

Clothing also was not plentiful. Clothes were always handed down from the older child to the next in line. "I never had a suit of clothes in the old country," Papa said. "I always had pants through my brother and a jacket, and things like that." Shoes were worn by the children to go to church, school, and during the winter months only. These also were handed down to the next sibling in line. "Well, we get used to it, to walk around with no shoes," he said. "In spring, of course, our feet were all smashed up, bumping on the stones and things like that. It was not too good in the beginning of spring, and then you get used to it and be done with it."

Young brides were expected to know how to sew all the family clothes. However, the one dress suit a grown man owned was made by a tailor in town. Girls learned clothing design and sewing in school before they graduated at age fourteen. If a woman couldn't sew well, she was helped by another woman who could. Once a year, the women of Cloz would travel together to Clez, a town approximately five miles away, to buy the sewing fabrics they needed for the year. If they did not spin their own yarn, they bought yarn to knit the winter socks. Knitting was done during spare time in warm summer months.

World War I would create all kinds of shortages of goods. There was little or no fabric or even thread to buy. Papa's mother, Maria, would spin her own coarse flax thread on a hand-held spindle, using the flax she grew on a small plot of ground. This thread was used for mending rough-textured work clothes because of its coarseness. Women had to undo clothing in order to sew anything new that was needed or to retrieve some mending thread. They washed clothes carefully so as to not wear them out.

During the war, soap was costly and impossible to buy, so the women made soap of soda, lye, and rendered fat. Only coarse, rough clothes could be washed with it because it would burn lighter, more delicate fabrics. Whatever store-bought soap they had was carefully and sparingly used for delicates and shirt collars and cuffs. Women had a lot of hard work to do.

Papa's mother was indeed hard-working, kind, and generous. Like many of the other women, she often worked in the fields after getting her children settled in the morning. Always, but especially in the very hard years, she shared what she had with those who were poorer. She was a well-liked woman who was humorous but quiet and reserved, a peace-maker who would smooth over arguments, always protecting love and communication in the family. Her children learned this well from her because I saw this trait in my father and his sister, Gelinda. Maria was a woman of dignity who never gossiped.

All these traits Papa proudly described in his mother. She was known to support and encourage her children, but was also the disciplinarian of the family since Archangelo was always busy working the farm. He, however, took care of serious matters, such as any difficulty with morals and values, Papa said. Decisions were made together but he had the last say when they disagreed.

I think Papa may have inherited his love of humor from his mother because of a story he told of her. It seems that the ladies would set out a table in the piazza between the houses and bring out samples of their cooking to taste and share recipes. As I mentioned before, seldom did anyone have even a very small amount of meat or fowl to cook. When it was time for Maria to leave the group, she would quip, “I have a big veal roast in the oven. I better go home before I burn it.” Besides her humor and compassion, she could be quite exacting. She also watched carefully over the family money and was not too free with it. I imagine with nine children she had good reason.

Papa’s father, Archangelo, was also a compassionate person, and understanding, but a strict man. Being strict was part of the male culture. He was a man who had great insight and common sense, a trait I’ve admired in my father. Archangelo was highly respected because of this, and he worked for the good of their small town of sixteen-hundred people.

But he was also good-natured. This rugged, medium-built farmer with his chiseled face, thinning hair and dark moustache, also liked fun. In the winter months when farm work was minimal, he enjoyed card games with the men at their local bar, which was more a gathering place than a drinking place. Occasionally, he liked to bring his friends home to his wine cellar for a drink. Maria decided this was using up the family’s needed supply of wine, so on one occasion she locked up the cellar. Grandpa simply broke the lock, and that was the end of that!

This family picture shows Papa (in back row, at right) with his parents and siblings.

CHAPTER 2

CHORES, SCHOOL, TALENT AND GRIEF

Papa started his life stories at about age ten. He began with, "In the morning I used to be getting up about six o'clock, make the fire in the wood-burning side of the stove with pine cones. We used to be letting the pine cones sit on top of the stove overnight to let them dry out, then they're good for starting a fire. Then I get the water and put it in the coffeepot and put it on the stove for the chicory coffee. After that I wake up Gelinda, my sister, to cook the patate rostede. Before breakfast I was helping my father to milking one cow." He is speaking here of his morning chores before school. Papa was a handsome boy, husky-framed with dark, thick, wavy, reddish-brown hair and hazel eyes. He was already trained and capable of doing farm chores, but was also fun-loving and mischievous.

When still in his preteen years, his parents were both sick with the flu so he had to attend to their livestock. After starting the fire in the stove and putting on the coffee water, he would milk all the cows, then bring the milk to the dairy where it was purchased for the production of cheese (a staple food for these mountain people). Returning to the barn, he would give water and feed to the cattle, go inside to wash up and eat breakfast, getting to school as soon as possible but usually late.

At noon he fed the cattle, ate his lunch and returned to school. In the evening, he again milked the cows, brought the milk to the cheese-maker, again went to the fountain for water, giving the cows water and bedding for the night. Papa accepted the yoke of a heavy workload at a very young age. This became the story of his life. Actually, it gave him a fiercely strong body which, combined with his personal strengths, enabled him to continue working until he was eighty-nine.

During this particular time, one of his enduring personality traits became evident. He would always tolerate situations for just so long, then he would say, "Basta!" which meant "Enough!" after which he would take necessary action. During his parents' illness, he said that one day he became tired or upset – discouraged, I guess. To make matters worse, one of the cows was hard to milk and ticklish. She kept swishing Papa's face with her tail. He, in turn, tried to pin her tail between his knee and her hind leg, but she would get it loose and kept swishing his face. "Finally I got mad," he said, "and I bit um. I bite the teat, you know. She give me a kick and she throw me out of the barn, milk and all."

I asked him why he had to do so much work when he had three brothers and five sisters. His matter-of-fact reply showed that he didn't consider the responsibility put on him as unjust. He explained that Stephan, his older brother, was away at school. Stephan eventually became a professor, a Doctor of Literature, and twice won an international prize for Latin poetry. He also spoke five languages fluently. Papa said that during the early mornings when he was sent up the slopes to check on their grape crops, he would sometimes find Stephan sitting under the grape-laden trellises contemplating and writing poetry about the sunrise over their beautiful mountains and valley.

The girls did mostly the inside work. His brother, Romano, who would later take over the farm duties, was a little boy, and the youngest, Lino, was only an infant. Lino left the family home forever at age eleven to enter the seminary, also achieving high academic honors and mastering five languages. Because of his intelligence, he was prepared and given permission to be ordained into the Franciscan Order two years early, at the age of twenty-three.

Not only did my father, Joseph, shoulder the responsibility of being his father's helper, but he also felt inadequate by comparison to his intelligent brothers. School was difficult for him. His chores took too much time away from study. Also, he could not distinguish between certain sounds such as the letters V and F, and math memorization eluded him. These signs of dyslexia are clear today but were unknown at that time. Resigned to his fate, Papa would write out his math table in advance whenever he had time, knowing his teacher would give him this as a punishment for failure to recite them correctly. "I was not made for study; I was made for work," Papa said, with a resignation in his tone of voice. You could hear grief in the pronouncement of his destiny. Papa's school problems also made his dream of becoming a priest impossible. He would often say, "I was just too dumb." Instead, he worked for the church his entire life, which enabled him to serve God as best he could.

In his final years, hopefully I may have gotten him to understand and believe that his obvious keen intelligence was evident in the way he handled the often tricky or difficult events of life and that his school problems were only a matter of dyslexia. Because it is said to be hereditary, history has repeated itself. Some of Papa's children and grandchildren have this learning disability as well, and everyone who does has succeeded despite it, due to today's awareness of the problem.

Papa continued his childhood story with a happy memory of when he was eleven-years-old. His father bought lumber at the top of the mountain's forest line to build a new barn. One day he told Papa that they would be going up to get the lumber. It took about six or seven trips up the mountain to complete the job. They would leave at two o'clock in the morning, his father taking the shortcut to get there ahead of time to prepare the load, while Papa took the regular route with the cattle-drawn car, arriving at about six o'clock. They would load up and start back down, getting to their farm at about ten o'clock in the morning.

One day was particularly humid. Papa was anxious to get to his father at the destination point because something strange was happening to his body and he was afraid. As soon as he saw his father, he told him he was sick. "But you don't look sick, Joseph," Archangelo said. "I am sick, Father!" Papa insisted. "Water is coming all over me, coming out!"

His father asked, "Has this ever happened to you before, Joseph?" When Papa said no, he said his father smiled broadly, telling him it would happen many more times during his life. Papa grinned happily as he told of this event and ended by saying, "It was my first time sweating." I suspect his smile at that moment wasn't born just out of humor but that this was obviously a fond memory of his father.

Still in his young years, Papa dealt with another frightening situation. It was the fall of 1912 when his older brother Stephan, a tall, lean, very handsome young man, was returning to college. At that time, college came after they graduated from lower education at age fourteen. Stephan had to go to Clez to catch a railcar which would take him to the train station in the large and ancient city of Trento. The railcar was like the streetcars of the United States. Both the railcar and the train were constructed mostly of wood, affording little comfort. Clez was a long ride by cattle-drawn cart through the mountain passes.

That morning, Papa got up at one o'clock in the morning, loaded Stephan's trunk onto the cart which he hitched up to one of their cows. Once loaded up, he started off to Clez with the trunk. Stephan slept a while longer and then took the shortcut by foot, arriving at the depot on time for the four o'clock in the morning railcar. The trip to the depot in the dark didn't scare Papa but for some reason the return trip did. The road led up over a mountain, through both forest and rocky areas.

At one point of the journey it was necessary to cross a bridge suspended over a gorge. The gorge was so deep that the river at its bottom could be heard but barely seen. Stories were often told of thieves waiting on this bridge and even shoving one of their victims off into the gorge. "I was young, only thirteen," Papa said, "and kind of scared, so I put myself in the cart and covered myself with the straw. I had a pocket knife, you know, and I take it out and hold it." At thirteen, he was going to defend himself with that pocket knife. Carefully hidden under the straw, he soon fell asleep, lulled by the swaying cart while the cow instinctively found its way back to the barn.

Of all the stories I will write about Papa, this next one is the most difficult for me. When I think of it, I again see my father as he would tell this story from time to time. He would always be quiet in his telling, his shoulders always drooped and there was a sadness in his voice. No anger, just sadness. I loved him so much that I grieved with him and grieved for the child in him who had to endure the pain which would forever scar his heart and affect his status in Cloz. It also greatly influenced his great compassion and respect of children.

This situation happened the summer before and during his last year of school. As I mentioned before, mandatory education ended at age fourteen in those days, but the education level was equivalent to high school. Despite some learning difficulties, Papa got along well in school because he was always well behaved. His parents, especially his father, expected a grade of one in conduct and a one or two in religion from all the children. Respect for authority in school as well as at home, and all authority in general was a must.

A vengeance against Papa's father was the cause of this event in Papa's life. His father, Archangelo, was a trustee of the town. Because he was a man of high integrity and intelligence, the people often tried to make him mayor, a position he accepted once. As trustee, he was greatly involved with school matters and at times had strong disagreements with the teachers. Archangelo fought for what was good for the school and the students. As Papa explained, "My father was a very strict man. He was a man of few words, but before talking he was thinking twice. When he said a word, that was the word." Papa's teacher, in particular, was at great odds with Archangelo.

It all started in late spring. The older students were dismissed from school a month earlier than the rest of the children so they could help with spring planting. A couple of boys pulled a vicious prank on Papa's teacher and, when caught, they implicated Papa as having been with them. As far as I could understand, these boys had gotten into the teacher's home and had broken things. "One of them was a very bad boy who later became a thief," Papa said.

At the time of the incident, Papa was grazing cows in a pasture some distance up the mountain with a neighbor boy. Only the most trustworthy boys in town were allowed to take all the cattle from the town farms up the mountain to graze on better wild grass. He and Silvio, a boy who lived near him, were chosen for this honorable job. Because the cattle were so contented they decided not to come down the mountain that day for lunch. They picked wild strawberries to eat instead, staying in the pasture all day.

The next day, Papa heard he had been accused of the vandalism. He immediately went to his teacher to defend his innocence, giving reliable proof and a witness. His teacher refused to listen to him, saying, "Joe, I don't want to hear anything. Just come back to school in September." Papa protested. "But teacher, this is the time to make this trouble stop." His teacher repeated that he wasn't interested in anything my father had to say. "At age fourteen, boys were not children but men," Papa said, and he tried to defend himself as a man but it was of no use.

In September, on the first day of school, Papa took his assigned seat in the back of the classroom. Back seats were for quiet, well-behaved students. The front seats were reserved for the "wild kids." Before prayers were said, the teacher called Papa to his desk and told him to kneel down. Papa asked, "For what?" The teacher just repeated, "Kneel down." Papa again insisted, "I want to know why I have to kneel down." The teacher replied, "For what you did this summer." "Well," Papa said, "I came in the next day that the thing happened and I explained to you but you didn't want to listen, and what I say to you is the truth." "Kneel down," repeated the teacher.

Papa knelt beside the teacher's desk until lunch. Upon their return to class in the afternoon, the teacher again made Papa kneel. When the other children were dismissed for the day, he was not allowed to get up. His father had told him not to stop anywhere after school, to get home immediately because they had to plow one of the fields. He begged his teacher, "Give me any punishment you want but let me go because my father's waiting for me to plow the field." The teacher replied, "Stay kneeling." He kept Papa kneeling until five o'clock. When he finally let him get up and leave, the teacher gave Papa a slip of paper with a bad conduct report on it which Papa would have to have his father sign.

At supper time that night, he gave the slip to his father. Trustingly, he said, "Father, I was punished for what happened to the teacher's home this summer. I explained it to you, it's not the truth. I was grazing the cows all that day with Silvio who knows the truth." The sadness and softness in Archangelo's face and his tone of voice both told Papa that his father knew very well of his innocence and that he was not angry at Papa. He could tell his father felt badly about the unjust treatment he had received, knowing it was political revenge against himself. But in keeping with the belief that authority was not to be questioned and must be strictly obeyed, Archangelo did not take Papa's side or support him. He said, "Joe, come here by me and kneel down." He did this as an example for the rest of the children that the teacher's authority is not questioned. Papa understood.

This sad event did not end here. On the last day of school, students graduating went up to the teacher's desk. He said a few words and then gave them their final report cards. No ceremony, no parties given afterward. These few moments brought a simple, uncelebrated end to their education. This report card was used when applying for higher education, jobs, political office or any position of trust. The conduct grade was of most importance. The teacher gave Papa a conduct grade of five. With a grade of five, a person would never have any job of responsibility, and it pretty much closed off any employment, schooling, or advancement that a person might seek. Papa said, "When I saw it I got a shock." He stared at it and then looked the teacher right in the eyes and said, "Remember, teacher, this five in conduct will never go out of my mind. You know it's unjust."

Years later, one of Papa's teachers was visiting the United States. Papa told her about this incident and she said that Papa's teacher could not arbitrarily give the five in conduct without first going to the highest authority of the school and with the knowledge of the other teachers, which she knew he did not do since she was there at the time. He evidently took it upon himself and for his own purposes, and without authority gave Papa that five. Leaving the country to go to America at the age of twenty-one, Papa said that the five in conduct went with him painfully in his heart.

Papa's young life also held a lot of happiness. Among the things he found so enjoyable in his teen years were the plays he performed in during long, snowbound winter months when farm chores were few. As I mentioned before, the plays were held in the church hall, which was the center of social life in Cloz.

The actors did all the necessary jobs in putting on the performances. At times, Papa would take tickets at the door. Children who were too poor to even afford the small admission would stand at the entrance peering in with disappointment and longing. My father would look the other way while taking them by the hand and pulling them in behind his back, then pushing them into the audience unseen. In Papa's old age, a fellow countryman thanked him for this kindness of seventy years past. These performances would be announced in church after Sunday Mass and all the townspeople usually came to see the show.

Papa's first stage-fright happened when at age fourteen he performed in a play called *The Two Sergeants*. It was based on a true story about treason, a duchess of Venice, and royal officials. His brother, Stephan, was on a college break and was the director as well as acting in two roles. It was a difficult play.

Stephan wanted them to understand the characters so that the actors could portray them well. Papa explained, "If you want to make a good part you have to know the man the way he is." Stephan gathered the actors and did a read-through of the play. He then gave them all the history and background of the story. As Papa said, "Without knowing it, we were learning history, too."

The boys took both the male and female parts as it was considered "not nice" for girls to be performing on stage. When the play was ready they did three performances to accommodate all the townspeople.

Papa's part in this play was that of the "bad guy" and while waiting to go on, Papa made the mistake of peeking through the stage curtains and saw that the hall was packed. He froze. His mind went blank. The entrance onto the stage was small and the area backstage was dark. Papa tried to look in his play book and though he was staring at the words, he couldn't read the lines. He pleaded with Stephan, "I can't make it. I can't go out. I can't remember one word of my part."

Stephan was rushing around with behind-the-scenes details but stopped long enough to give Papa something strong to drink. "I don't know what it was," Papa laughed, and then said that his entrance cue lines were spoken on stage and he stood frozen in front of the door. Stephan gave him a strong shove and Papa was on stage. Stephan repeatedly was giving him his first line from backstage. Papa said, "The first word wouldn't come out of my mouth. It was stuck. I started to sweat." He stood there staring at the other actors. Finally the words came. As it turned out, that fierce staring pause was perfect for the scene because he entered at a moment in the play where he catches the officials plotting against him.

At the end of the play, Papa's character was humiliated and stripped of his gun, medals and badges. With that, the young kids sitting in the front row started shouting, "There, Joe, now you got what you deserve!" The audience often reacted and almost interacted with the performance. Grinning, Papa remembered, "I had to bite hard on my tongue to cause pain so I could keep from laughing."

He also recalled a scene from another play where he was shot. He had a cow's intestine sack filled with cow's blood hidden inside his clothes, which he squeezed when he was shot. Blood gushed out all over his clothes. His little brother Lino ran up to the stage screaming, "They killed Joe!"

In all, Papa performed in about five plays before leaving Cloz. Because of his strong build and serious looking face, he usually took the part of the villain or austere man.

CHAPTER 3

WAR, STARVATION AND TRAIN ROBBERY

On June 28, 1914, World War I began. Papa had just graduated from school. He was not quite fifteen. All able-bodied men between the ages of seventeen and forty were drafted into the army. War was fearsome to the young boys who lived in these quiet little mountain towns who knew no violence and killing. At first, Papa was too young to be drafted but he was called upon to help with the war effort.

At the beginning of the war, Papa's father was drafted into the army, and his uncle, also a farmer, was ill. So Papa ran both farms for a long while, doing all the main farm work. On Sundays, or if there was ever any time on a weekday evening, he and a group of his friends would cut hay for women who had to tend their farms alone because their husbands and sons were off to war. To the day he died, Papa would always insist, "For God, never work on Sunday for profit. Only work if it's to help the poor and needy."

As the war progressed, young men between the ages of fifteen and seventeen were randomly picked for various jobs necessary for the war effort. This was mandatory labor if you were selected. Because he had always worked hard, Papa's five-foot, ten-inch frame was strong and he was very capable. Papa was always being picked. Usually the job was bringing trees down the mountain, taking them to a sawmill, and then delivering the lumber to wherever fortifications were being built.

At other times, he and another boy were sent to the "powder house" to get dynamite. Actually, it was a cave built into the mountainside. They had to remove their outer clothes and shoes, then put on rubber boots and special garments without buttons. This was to prevent the buttons or nails in the soles of their shoes from accidentally scraping on the rocks, thus causing a spark which might ignite the dynamite. They would load the explosives into backpacks and carry them long distances to wherever rock needed to be blown out in order to build fortifications into sides of mountains.

Within days of his return home after one of his war jobs, he would be picked again. He was unable to get his own family's farm chores done or earn much needed money for his family. Finally, at age sixteen, he packed his suitcase and left Cloz. He went to another valley where young men were not being selected for war labor. There he found a job working for "a very good family," he said, and was able to earn money to send home. This family grew fruit and made wine and whiskey with it. First Papa helped bring in the grape harvest and then he worked in the winery.

After the grapes were crushed, extracting the juice to make wine, the residue was used to make whiskey. In Papa's words, "After we got wine out, we make whiskey. Boil it and ferment it. Day after All Saints Day, November first, the boiler is going day and night. Christmas Eve to the twenty-sixth the boiler was closed, then started up again." He worked long hours.

Papa remembered that the foreman was a good man. He also said, "The foreman drank more wine than he could carry. Never drunk – red face like fire but never walking zig-zag." The foreman went from barrel to barrel sampling the wine and had Papa try some from a particularly long barrel. He asked Papa if he liked it, and Papa said he did. Teasingly he informed my father that the wine from that barrel was made for women.

Papa shot back, "Since you're drinking it so much, are you a woman?!"

At one point, the foreman instructed Papa to check one of the vats. As he lifted the cover off the vat, he was overcome by the alcohol fumes, almost falling into the vat. He scrambled down from the platform surrounding the huge vat and was able to get out into the fresh air. When feeling better, he looked for his foreman and asked for a rope to tie around his waist, insisting on having the foreman on the other end of the rope for safety. He wasn't afraid to speak up when necessary. Using common sense was always his approach to life.

Unlike his fellow workers and countrymen in general, Papa didn't drink wine with his meals. The teasing he got because of this didn't bother him, he said, and the employer's daughters soon learned to provide coffee for his lunch. Their lunch consisted of bread, cheese, sausage, bacon, and fruit.

Papa never drank alcohol except on very rare occasions. Finally, in his eighties, he drank some brandy at times when he had chest pain from his ailing heart. However, until he was in

In this 1916 picture, Papa, seated at the left, is shown with fellow soldiers.

his seventies he continued to make whiskey to have on hand for guests or in case of sickness. Most, if not all, of his countrymen who came to America did, too. Some made wine also. During prohibition in the United States their wine and whiskey-making caused confrontations with the law, and some were arrested. When I talk of Papa's early days in America, I'll tell you how he managed to get the local authorities to leave them alone.

In 1916, Papa's days of working at the winery were over. At age seventeen my father, Joseph, was drafted into the army. "I was eighteen months in Russia. The Russian front." He said, "We was in Bohemia and Prague in Czechoslovakia to get the training. We have to go through Poland where we stayed for a while and then little by little we got to the Russian border." They were issued a metal helmet called a berndorfer. When necessary, they removed one piece of clothing at a time to wash, doing without that piece until it was dry. They lived with dirt and lice for the duration of the war. When he returned home in 1918, getting rid of his lice was the first order of business.

However, lice and dirt were not the worst difficulty of war; hunger was. As the war continued, there were conditions of starvation which grew steadily worse. In Papa's words, "This was the condition – Austria and Germany, they was closed in. They had no port to get the stuff in because Italy went against Austria and the only place the boats come in was through Italy. Austria and Germany did not have seaports. They had food but not enough food for four years. This was one of the main reasons for their loss of the war. Austria took inventory of the food on all the farms in the country and found that there was only enough left for four more months and the winter was coming, so they gave up the war."

When I asked my father about this lack of food, how they managed to get any, he hesitated and finally said, "I don't want to go through all the details of that. In only a short way I tell you this. The hunger was very bad and I was two times at the point of starvation, but especially one time. I was twenty-six days without seeing the kitchen. Without anything. It was springtime. There was nothing to steal on the farms. Sometime we had food, otherwise we had to beg for food, steal it, or pick through garbage for potato peelings or whatever we could find. In spring, that's all there was, was cherries." He then went on to tell this story.

His squad had managed to take control of a small Russian town which bordered Poland. In guarding the Russian border, "The people's revolution was often worse than the war," he said. Since there were only a few of them, they stayed inside a building, doing various maneuvers to give the townspeople the impression that there were many of them. They knew that if their small number of men were known, they would soon be captured. If they purchased food, the shopkeepers would know the quantity was for only a few men. Their only means of obtaining food was stealing cherries under the cover of darkness.

It was my father's turn to go out looking for cherries. The only trees he could find were clustered around a farmhouse which was about a mile down the road, on the Polish side of the border. At three o'clock in the morning, using trees and shrubs for cover because the moon was bright, he stole his way carefully along the road leading out of town. Crossing a small bridge, he entered the farm.

Climbing one of the trees, he groped in the darkness for cherries, filling his backpack for the other men. Then he began frantically eating his fill for the day. He was so hungry that he forgot to watch for the sunrise, concentrating instead on eating as much as he possibly could. The sky began to lighten; night had given way to morning. He stayed too long and now risked exposing his squad's ploy, possibly causing their capture. He began to quickly climb down the tree when the farmer came out of the house.

Papa said farmers in that area always left their houses with a hatchet or very long stick in hand to either do work or protect themselves. The old, white-haired man took his long fruit harvesting stick in hand, which was leaning against the house. Because he was only about ten yards from the tree, he saw my father climbing down and he immediately pointed his stick at Papa. While clinging to the tree, Papa drew his bayonet, ready to use it if necessary. He said he didn't want to, but figured he'd have to if the farmer attacked.

When I asked him about his use of the bayonet, he said in a troubled way, "We were proficient in using the bayonet. I was good in throwing the bayonet. In the army we were taught not to hurt anybody, but to defend ourselves. That's all I want to say about it."

He and the farmer just stared at each other, motionless, for a long time. There was enough morning light for Papa to see tears rolling down the man's face. At that moment my father knew that the farmer would not hurt him. He slid down the tree and ran as fast as he could. Luckily, reinforcements came that day. His squad went home for a short furlough.

While he was home, there were Polish soldiers begging for food in his town. Papa said, "There was a boy who lived close to me, my age, but he never went into the army. He was too small or sick or something. A Polish soldier went up to him to ask for some food. He started to holler at the soldier. I got tied-up inside and I go over and say, 'Listen, if you got nothing to give to him, don't holler at the man because it's not fun to go out and beg for something to eat.' Then I say to the soldier in Polish, 'Come over to my home, maybe my mother has something.' She bring out some potatoes, polenta, and a cruet of wine and he eat." (Because of his war experiences, Papa could speak some German, Russian, and Polish.) Papa's family invited the young soldier to their home every night for the supper meal, explaining that they were poor but there was always enough soup and an extra potato for him.

One night after supper as they exchanged war experiences, Papa told the Polish soldier about the cherry tree incident. The young man seemed more and more excited as he listened and then began to anxiously ask questions. "Was it a white farm house? Was it about a mile out of town? Was there a small bridge to cross just before coming to the farm? Did the farmer have white hair?" All Papa could say was, "Yes, yes, yes." The soldier replied, "That was my father." Papa then understood the old man's tears. After that revelation, Papa said, "Anyway, we got not like soldiers but like brothers."

Several nights later, at about two o'clock in the morning, there was loud calling and pounding at the front door. It was the young soldier, explaining that his company was leaving town. He asked Papa to please bring a letter to his father telling him that he was alive and well and that he loved him. The two young soldiers promised to stay in touch, but my father never heard from the Polish soldier again. With that quiet sense of fate in his voice, Papa said, "Well, many got killed, you know."

Papa's squad was not sent back to that Russian/Polish border town. Unable to personally deliver the letter, Papa wrote a description of the farm and its location under the man's name on the envelope and mailed it, forever hoping it was received by the old farmer.

The starvation endured during the war years deeply affected Papa. He could never throw food away. Many times, when Mama cooked too much, he would bring the leftovers to my home, saying, "If you can use it for the family, that's good; otherwise throw it away. I can't."

To help the men cope with their hunger and other rigors of

war, the Austrian army gave the soldiers four cigarettes a day, or the making for the same, which the men would roll into thinner cigarettes, thus increasing their number of cigarettes, or they were given pipe tobacco. Papa didn't smoke. Every second or third day, they were given a slice of bread of which Papa said, "It was as big as a hand and so thin you could see through it." He would trade his cigarettes for bread. "I always kept a dried piece of bread in my pocket for when I was sure I was going to die of starving, then I would have it to eat and stay alive. I kept it, too, in case I met up with my father, to give it to him."

Because of the hunger, Papa finally learned to smoke. He tells the story this way. "Once we had a long walk, they call it a security march. Around nine o'clock at night we stopped and I laid down. I was so hungry and weak I couldn't get up. My partner say, 'Joe, why don't you smoke? It takes away that feeling of hungry.' I say, 'But what does that smoke have to do with hunger?' He say, 'Just try it, Joe.' So I did try smoking and I got sick like a dog. I was sweating cold and my legs were trembling. I couldn't get up."

The trumpet sounded the call to resume the march but he was unable to stand. He told his partner absolutely not to tell what had just happened. When his Sergeant asked why he was lying there, Papa innocently replied, "I'm sick, I can't stand." The Red Cross was sent to administer medication and to give him a ride back while the men finished the last two-and-a-half hours of march. He told this last part with a chuckle in his voice.

After that, he gradually began smoking to calm the hunger. One of the older soldiers also taught him to whistle to distract himself when the emptiness and pain in his stomach was too great. To cope with war, the soldiers would also sing in harmony and yodel, both of which Alpine people do so beautifully. The supportive camaraderie between the soldiers also helped.

Unfortunately, comaraderie wasn't always the way of the soldiers. Some of the men discovered that Papa was extremely ticklish, so a couple men grabbed him and held him down, while another man tickled Papa until he literally became crazed. Breaking free from their grips, he grabbed is rifle and aimed it at the offenders and was ready to shoot when their sergeant appeared at the door. The offending men were severely punished.

Papa ended his stories of war-time hunger with this next incident. With deep sadness and a welling of tears in his eyes, my father recalled the story of one of the soldiers in his squad who found some potato peelings and the bottoms of some root plants in a garbage pile, which he was boiling in his helmet. The heavy, round, metal helmets made perfect cooking pots. Accidentally, the helmet was tipped over, spilling this precious soup of garbage – picked peelings and scraps. The man became frantic. He got down on his knees and licked up the spilled soup from the floor. Papa was silent for a while after telling this story. That memory of seventy-three years in his past still painfully gripped his heart and soul.

Along with the hunger, the soldiers also endured fleas and body lice, as I mentioned before. On one bitterly cold night, with temperatures well below freezing, Papa decided to freeze those bugs to death. He washed out his undershirt the best he could, then hung it out in the freezing cold. Hours later he retrieved his shirt, which was frozen like a board. Papa said, "As soon as my shirt thawed out, those little bugs started moving around again. The cold didn't kill them!"

Papa continued on with his war stories. He told the following story in these words: "We had a Sergeant who was very good, like a father to us, but he was very strict. When he say to do this, you got to do it the way he say, otherwise he was very severe. Mostly, he was treating you like a father."

Papa went on to say that when they entered a town, the soldiers would sleep in the homes of the townspeople in groups of two or three per house. They had no other sleeping accommodations when in the towns, and the people were obliged to give them shelter. The women of the house had to rid the house of lice when they left. Papa was always in the Sergeant's group and shared a bedroom with him.

"One day," Papa continued, "I was at my guard post. I was guarding a butcher shop where they were butchering for the soldiers and for the town. I remember it was from one to three o'clock in the morning. It was a night foggy and dark, you couldn't see hardly one step. I saw something coming along, something moving, you know. I say, 'Halt,' and he stop. He wasn't moving anymore so I was watching, and then he was moving again.

I say 'Halt' again. When you say halt the second time you get your gun off the shoulder and point it up, then when you say halt the third time you point the gun at the person. When he come along the third time, I say, 'Halt' and he didn't stop so I pointed the gun. He was a few yards away. He said, 'I'm the officer of the day,' and I know it was him, my Sergeant. 'Come along,' I say, but he have to stop three steps away from you. He never supposed to come close to you – three steps away.

But he come close and I moved my gun that had a bayonet on it and I nearly cut his ear off with the bayonet. He says, 'Joe, it's me.' I said, 'Three steps away,' because I don't know if he went out crazy or he was drunk or what he was trying to do. 'Okay, Joe,' he says, 'Cool off.' So I put my gun down, holding it with the end down on the ground. He says, 'Joe, let me see your gun,' and he reach for the gun to put a hand on it. I backed up and pointed the gun again. 'Joe,' he say, 'I want to see your gun.' 'If you want to see my gun,' I say, 'go get another soldier to change my guard. I don't care who you are.'

I told him, 'This is the law, this is my order.' So then he says, 'Okay, Joe,' and he cut it off. Then we start to talk." His officer told him that he had taken guns away from three other guards, even unloading their bullets. He thought that since Papa shared sleeping quarters with him and was like a trusted son to him, he was sure Papa would hand over his gun. Then he said, "Wait until tomorrow. These other guards should be court martialed."

The next afternoon, after a noon meal of tripe and weak coffee, all the men were told to load up in full gear, which meant an eighty-five pound pack on their backs. Papa was told to sit while the other men were made to do calisthenics until they were exhausted. The Sergeant then turned to Papa and commanded him, "Joe, you see that big rock in the field? That rock is the safety box of the regiment. Be sure to guard it."

After Papa took his post, the officer again tried to take Papa's gun. Unable to do so, he turned to the other men and told them that Papa was like a son to him and yet he was the only one he could not disarm the night before. Then he said, "This is why I punished all of you today. If it had been another officer of the day, you would all have been arrested and court martialed."

Having talked so much about guns, I asked my father if he was involved in a lot of combat, a lot of actual fighting. He said, "Not exactly the fighting. I was in where there was revolution, where the people was uprising. That was worst than the fighting. We was always in the front. There was no fighting in the front. We was sleeping under the ground in the trenches, you know. We was making rooms under the ground." Then I asked him if he had to shoot bullets during the uprisings and also when he was on the guard. He didn't want to elaborate on this. I didn't push into his private war memories.

My father was in the army for eighteen months and now

close to nineteen years of age when the First World War ended. Papa said, "The Captain come along one morning and says, 'From this minute on, I'm not your officer no more because Austria gave up the war.' Austria gave up not because we are defeated but because we have not enough to eat. The Captain continued, 'Don't forget, we are far away from home and you need a leader to go home, so between you, select a man you want to lead you to take you home.'" Papa said, "We were in Russia, we could not walk home. So we selected a Lieutenant, a very good man, and by this Lieutenant he was selecting me and another two guys to help him. So we do the arrangements." The men had to provide their own transportation home. The military did not provide for this.

The four men found four empty train cars on a track. It was a three-hour walk into the town that had a depot. They took the few horses they had and rode in to find an engine and engineer to pull the four cars they found, but were told that all the engines were being used to take other soldiers home.

On the following days they kept getting the same answer. Knowing that one of their group was a train fireman who knew how to drive an engine, they decided to take matters into their own hands. They decided to steal a train engine. They had to get out of Russia. The war had ended eight days before and none of their families knew if they were alive. Soldiers had been arriving home for days already.

"We went into town," Papa said, "and watched until one engine was loose or out and gonna go up and steal it even if there is a man in it. We went into the depot and, sure enough, one machine was there. Just the engine, no cars. We went over and talked nice to this guy and asked him to come pull us, but he say no. He had to go pull other cars of soldiers. We pulled out our guns and told him either come out to get us with our four cars or get off the train, so he get off. We took the engine."

About a block down, the tracks turned. Until they cleared the depot and the surrounding area, Papa said they knew they might be shot at, but they made it safely.

Back at their camp, they kept the engine under constant guard until they finished breaking up camp. Keeping only enough guns and ammunition for each man to carry, they threw the rest into a deep water well so that no one else could use them. They hooked up the four cars loaded with their men and equipment and drove it into the depot. They parked right in front of the main doors of the depot.

They were on the main line which controlled traffic entering and leaving the depot. Entering the building, they found the same man who had refused to help them. They announced, "Your machine and four cars are outside." "Oh, you're the guys who stole the engine," the man said. "We are the guys," Papa said. "Here is your machine and here we are." "But you cannot go any farther," the man said. "Well, if you want to use this line, you're going to have to connect us to somebody," Papa said. They had the depot blocked with four cars of armed men. Finally, an already heavily-loaded train came by and despite protests that it could not pull any more cars, they connected the four cars and took my father's company to Vienna.

Before reaching Vienna, they had to cross several borders and each time had to comply with that country's regulations. Their guns were taken, two barrels of rum they carried for the men who had the flu were taken, and supplies were taken. As Papa put it, "We went through a lot of monkey business. It was tough. We had to pass through a lot of borders and each had its own laws."

The trip home caused a lot of deaths. Soldiers were so anxious to get home that they weren't thinking clearly of anything else. They clung onto the sides of train cars if they couldn't fit inside. They rode underneath where bums usually hitched rides and, worst of all, they rode on top of the cars. The train tunnels through the mountain passes were narrow and low. The men coming from small towns were unaware of this and were crushed to death as they went through the tunnels. Papa remembered sadly, "When you see the train coming you no see cars. That's all you see is people coming. They was hanging all over the cars. There was one good thing that happened. All through Europe, even though there was this revolution, the trains keep going. If there was a strike or something, it would have been a disaster."

Finally near their hometown, Cloz, Papa and a fellow soldier had to walk the last five miles. He recalled his homecoming in these words: "The families thought we probably were dead because the war ended two weeks before and we never come home. We was about a mile-and-a-half from Cloz where there was a river. We stop and I say, 'No more starvation. Now we can eat our bread.' So we take out our crust of bread we was always saving in case of starving and we dunk it into the river to make it soft, and we eat it. We ate our bread to say we were finished and safe now. It was three o'clock in the morning when I got home. I knocked on the door. I saw my sister jump up. They thought I was dead. My mother take a tub of water and a bar of soap and take all my clothes outside. They was full of lice."

With that simple and, I'm sure, joyful homecoming, Papa ended his war stories. Barely nineteen years old, Papa had already experienced so much hardship in life.

Our grandmother had vowed that if her son, Joseph, came home safe she would take him on a pilgrimage to a chapel of the Blessed Mother high in the Alpine mountains. It was a difficult road to travel and the last part of it had to be climbed by foot. It was the shrine of La Madonna de Piné. Papa and his mother fulfilled her promise in their journey there together.

CHAPTER 4

FIRST YEARS IN AMERICA

In the late 1800s and early 1900s, men from Cloz came to America to work in the coal mines for five or six years, made money, and then returned to their homeland and families. But many died in the mine accidents or returned to Cloz only to die of black lung disease which was so common among miners. Eventually, the Trentino area erected a large bronze statue depicting three miners in honor and memory of all the young men who went to America to work "in the hole."

After the First World War, the young men no longer wanted to die or get sick in the mines, so they started taking laboring jobs in the United States, even though it meant less pay. They earned just enough for their basic needs, which frustrated their hopes of sending money home to help their families. Then the Great Depression happened. Money and jobs were scarce. There was not enough money to travel back home to Cloz.

Gradually the young people began staying in America. The men would write to their hometown sweethearts. Some women eventually came to America to marry them. Whole families started coming also, and the young people met and married here. Their courtship was not dating as we know it. It was simply visiting a girl with her parents' permission in their home.

A couple of years after the war, Papa and a group of his bachelor friends decided that they, too, would leave for America. It was so hard on the parents to have their children go off into an unknown world, not knowing when or if they would see them again. Besides missing him, Papa had always been my grandparents' main helper on the farm and earning some income. But now Romano was old enough to help on the farm and the family was smaller. Stephan was away, continuing on with his studies and teaching; Gelinda was working as a domestic for a doctor's family in Milan, but the other sisters were now able to help at home and with farm chores. Little Lino entered the seminary at age eleven.

Several reasons caused my father to be willing to leave his beautiful land and the family he loved. There was that conduct grade of five which limited Papa's future, so he decided to try for something better in America and hopefully help his family financially by sending money home to them. Then there was the lingering memory of the starvation and horrors of war and the political climate that caused him to want to leave.

Now Papa knelt in the kitchen before the wood carving of the crucifixion and received his parents' blessing, which was their family's custom as the children left home to start their own lives. At age twenty-one, Papa was leaving for America, returning only once, about sixteen years later for a three-month visit. The grief of that goodbye was not only that they might not see each other again, but also that it would be months before my grandparents would know if Papa had arrived safely and was well situated in the United States. There were no telephones in Cloz, and mail was by slow ship and poor delivery.

This sense of separation and loss would sadly increase for Papa's parents when their thirteen-year-old daughter, Angelina, died of a burst appendix within a year after Papa left.

It was October 1920 when my father and his friends boarded a ship and began their long journey to Melrose Park, Illinois, to a new life. They chose this little Italian immigrant town because Father Benjamino Franch, a man from Cloz, was a missionary priest there at Our Lady of Mount Carmel Church. It is a town about fifteen miles west of Chicago.

They entered the United States on the shores of New York. Great crowds of immigrants filling the dock as they arrived were greeted by vendors, anxious to entice the travelers with food and American products after their long, tedious journey. One vendor in particular caught Papa's eye. Since he didn't arrive on a luxury ship and the voyage was three or four weeks long, there probably wasn't much, if any, fresh fruit on board. Papa noticed many people buying bunches of odd-looking, long, curved, yellow fruit from this vendor, so he figured they must be tasty. He bought some and bit into one, right through the skin of the fruit. Soft banana squished out and onto his clothes. It was many years before he ever ate a banana again.

When I asked my father what he thought of America when he first arrived, he laughed and said, "Hah, I was so surprised. When we was coming on the train from New York to Chicago we see the houses. I thought they was all chicken coops. The houses they was so small, you know. Over there, Cloz, the houses are not that way. They are big buildings. I thought they were all chicken coops! And then when we come to Melrose Park the houses were a little different. One thing I was so surprised was in a lot of houses they was put up a sign in the window, 'For Sale.' So for a week or so I was go around, walking, but I never go any farther than I could see the steeple of the church, you know, till I get used to it, the town. So I went by Father Franch one day and I say, 'Father, why they sell so much salt in this country?' He say, 'What you mean, Joe, they use so much salt?' Well, I tell him about a lot of houses they say for sale. In Italian, sale spells salt. Father Franch had a good laugh."

Speaking of houses, this was one of the first difficulties Papa and his friends encountered in this town they had chosen because no one wanted to rent an apartment to "those trouble-maker Austrians." The people of Melrose Park were almost entirely from Italy. Even though the people of Cloz were Italian-speaking and of Roman ancestry, they were Austrian citizens. The First World War had just ended a couple of years earlier in which the Austrians and Italians fought against each other, and sentiments were still strong. Turning for help to Father Franch, who then assured a homeowner that these were good young men, they finally found an apartment.

I would like to mention a little history at this point. At the northernmost border of Italy are the Alps, previously part of the Roman Empire. Cloz is located in the Alps. As a result of winning the First World War, Italy annexed or, you can say, reclaimed that area from Austria.

Having secured a place to live, they divided up the household and cooking chores. One of the men really didn't like housework but did play the accordion very well. After a few weeks of struggling with him to complete his job, he was reassigned a new job. He had to play the accordion all the while the others were cleaning house on Saturday. It made their work more enjoyable and everyone was happy with the arrangement.

Language was another problem. The people of Melrose Park were mostly from middle and southern Italy, while people from Cloz were from the farthest end of the now northern Italy. The dialects of the north and south were vastly different. They often couldn't understand one another. Papa tells of being in big trouble for several months and almost permanently losing newly made friends because of language.

He was invited to a party at his friend's home. A lot of young women were at the party, and when Papa arrived the party was lively and noisy. Papa said in Italian, "Que bordel!" meaning in his dialect, "What noise!" What he said in their dialect meant "What a house of prostitution!" Papa couldn't understand the offended and cool treatment he got from that point on. After a few months, Papa wanted to solve the problem and understand what was wrong, so he went to them and asked. This is typical of how Papa handled life. The matter was cleared up and Papa was very careful of his words after that.

Language was also a problem for Papa as he again experienced his old difficulty from school years – the difficulty of distinguishing between the sounds of certain letters of the alphabet. He and his bachelor friends decided to go downtown to Chicago for English classes. Papa wasn't able to learn English from the book or in class. After a while his teacher said, "Mr. Rauzi, you're going to have trouble. You cannot distinguish the sounds of words. For you it will be very hard." Papa's reply to the teacher was characteristic of his common sense and determination to do what he must do. "My friends will learn from books to speak English. I will go to the community and learn from the people." He did. He also learned to read and write, but his writing was often copying words prewritten for him.

As I mentioned before, household chores and cooking were shared by the men. Papa told the story of his friend Firmino's frustrating learning experience that involved baking cookies. One day, trying to make dunking cookies called "knots," his recipe was too loose, so he added flour. Then it was too stiff, so Firmino added liquid and butter. Now the batter was too soft again and couldn't be shaped by hand as needed – and so it went – too soft, too thick, too soft, too thick. His final batter had grown considerably and by the time Papa got home, Firmino had already baked a bushel full of cookies – literally a bushel full!

Papa went on to say that one day Firmino noticed a new picture Papa had in his wallet of his sister Gelinda. Firmino knew Gelinda but had not seen her for several years. He asked Papa if it would be alright to write to her. Papa knew Firmino to be a good man, a hard worker with a great sense of humor, so he gave his consent. Then he wrote to his parents and Gelinda to tell them about Firmino and the fact that he approved of him. Papa's judgment was then and always respected by his family – a fact that Gelinda emphasized in her late years.

After a letter courtship of about two years, Gelinda arrived in the United States. She stayed with some immigrant lady friends she knew from Cloz for two days preparing for her wedding. On May 11, 1924, she and Firmino were married at Our Lady of Mount Carmel Church. Theirs was a blessed and good marriage. They had ten children, all successful and very good people. Two became priests.

In her nineties, my aunt Gelinda said of my father: "How happy, how proud I am that we always loved and respected each other. There was never any unkindness between us." They lived not more than four miles from each other all their lives in the United States and their family bond, learned in childhood, remained strong.

Papa and some of the other men started their working years in America at Mount Carmel Cemetery in Hillside, Illinois, a town about nine miles from their flat in Melrose Park. Papa would bike to work. He was happy working at the cemetery, which he did for about twenty-seven years. Even though the pay wasn't much and there were no benefits, and working conditions weren't the best, he loved his work there. In the last years of life he said,

Papa is at the right in this picture, taken at the cemetery where he worked.

"Those were the happiest days of my life." It was working outside with the earth, grass, trees, flowers, and machinery; work that was familiar to him from his life in Cloz – work that was peaceful to him as well as being the humanitarian work of burying the dead.

He also worked side by side with Father Franch in building up the very young parish of Our Lady of Mount Carmel. He was instrumental in organizing and starting up most of their religious, social, and school groups. He was a member of the men's Holy Name Society and the Knights of Columbus, becoming a 4th degree Knight. For fifty years he was a leader for the big annual Feast of Our Lady of Mount Carmel. When he wasn't doing all these things, he was assisting Father Franch in any way needed, including serving at important dinners held at the parish rectory. Since in his heart he longed to be a priest, all of this work was a joy to him.

Before he had settled into these happier days, Papa had yet another sadness enter his life. The first three years in the United States were also very hard years for him. Having left behind the horrendous hardships of war, and the shame brought upon him by his teacher, he now lived a life of very hard work as a gravedigger for low wages and had to bicycle nine miles to work, even in the cold, snowy winter weather. He was poor and a long way from his family and beautiful homeland.

His mother sent him long, rusty brown, wool stockings which came up over his knees. She knit them so her son could keep his legs warm during harsh outside winter work. Years later, his mother-in-law, knowing how important these stockings were to him repaired them for Papa by knitting and attaching new soles, toes and heels to the original stockings which were worn away. Papa always kept them as a remembrance of his cemetery years and his mother's love and mother-in-law's kindness. Now I keep them.

Finally the war years and all the other hardships he endured took their toll. His young twenty-four-year-old heart, soul, and mind buckled under the strain. He began behaving and talking strangely. His friends suggested that he see a doctor. Finally the situation came to a head at work and his bosses fired him. They also committed him to a county hospital. With today's knowledge of mental health, his illness probably would be diagnosed as Posttraumatic Stress Disorder. Because of what seemed like his instability, the county started filing papers to have him deported. He was not yet a citizen of the United States.

Seeing the gravity of the situation, Father Franch and his friends hired the best lawyer they could find to prevent the deportation and to get him released from the hospital. In a number of weeks, a court hearing was held. The hospital stay was successful and the judge found Papa to be totally sane and ordered that he be released immediately and that all legal rights be restored to him.

That day was the Feast Day of Our Lady of Mount Carmel, which is very significant and explains Papa's life-long devotion to Our Lady of Mount Carmel. Papa returned to and forever remained his old self, steady and stalwart, a person others depended upon. The cemetery rehired him and Papa worked for them for another twenty-four years. They often asked

Papa can be seen here in front of the statue of Our lady of Mount Carmel, with his brother-in-law Mario and Fr. Benjamin franch.

Papa is seated at left, with his bachelor buddies from Cloz.

him to be a foreman, but he didn't want to be a boss; he just wanted to do his work, Papa said.

All was not hardship in Papa's life. He and his bachelor buddies from Cloz also enjoyed their lives and friendships in America. On one occasion, Papa suggested that they put on a play at the church hall "like the old country." They decided on a play in which Satan and an angel would fight over a man's soul. Papa played Satan and his character tried to tempt the man to steal from the church poor box. They had the stage rigged so that every time my father put his hand on a prop, a stagehand would reach through the backdrop and ignite smoke powder near Papa's hand. Smoke would puff up, giving him a very realistic satanic presence.

In the final scene, the man does steal from the church and as he leaves with his loot he is struck by lightning. The thunder was achieved by large sheets of metal backstage which were furiously shaken. The lightning was lit firecrackers being thrown across the stage. Satan claims the man's soul but from the other side of the stage a light is seen and as seven sheer curtains are slowly drawn away, the angel slowly appears in the light and says, "I'm not finished yet." With that, the almost dead man raises his head and begins praying.

Papa's character of Satan recoils to center stage where a reinforced circle had been cut out of the stage floor opening to the church's coalbin below. Satan, in a rage, says his final lines and the floor is released, dropping him into the coalbin where a stagehand had flames prepared in a container so that as Papa fell through the floor, flames shot up. For months after that the women in town avoided my father. His portrayal of Satan was just too realistic for them.

That play was followed by a fifteen-minute comedy routine to lighten up the people after that hour-long tense drama. The same cast did the comedy as well. This was followed by a second shorter play. Talk about getting your money's worth!

Movies were being made in Chicago in the 1920s and an agent happened to be in the audience for these performances. He convinced Papa to come into Chicago for a screen test, which he did. In his words, "When all those lights was on me and I heard the sound of the camera motors, I froze." He didn't

With his serious-looking face, Papa played
the part of the villian in plays.

regret failing at his chance for a movie career because he didn't approve of the lifestyle of actors, even though he greatly admired the talent of a good actor.

Papa always took the serious parts, as I mentioned before – the heavy, the villain. Despite his good looks, he had a very serious-looking face. I often wondered why I would be asked at times if my father was stern and strict. He was a good-natured man but his seriousness gave that impression. He explains it this way: "Well, about laughing, we was raised in a different way. Where I learned to laugh was in this country. If you say to me, 'How many times did you see your father laughing, doing a good laugh?' If you make me a millionaire, I could not say I did. He was a very good man but I never see him have a good laugh. He was all the time serious and the people were serious. They were raised like that."

Papa compared the seriousness of his people with the portrayal of Colonel Von Trapp in the movie *Sound of Music*, saying they were not regimented but of that seriousness. He also said that when his father said something, it was immediately obeyed; this was less so for his mother.

When pictures were sent back to the family in Cloz, great care was taken that no one would smile. It just wasn't considered dignified. Papa again emphasized that the people were not severe or mean. It was the commonly-held notion of the time that seriousness meant dignity and substantial character. That seriousness of face and intensity in an actor was also something Papa noticed and admired. All of his life he enjoyed watching a good actor perform. I remember many times when he was older, we would be watching TV and he would say, "Look at his face. Look how good he does his part." He would then decide what he thought the director was telling the actor to do.

CHAPTER 5

COURTSHIP AND MARRIAGE

My mother, Pauline, was about twelve-years-old when Papa left for America. She had seen him around Cloz but had never spoken to him. One day, her girlfriend knew Papa was working in the hayloft of a farm and convinced my mother to come with her to see him. The girls in town vied for his attention. He was very handsome and known to be a good guy. The girls were anxious to catch his eye. He was by then five-foot-ten, broad-shouldered, of strong build, and had dark, reddish-brown hair. Mama's girlfriend spoke to Papa for a couple of minutes. Mama, who was always a shy person, just stood by the doorway, watching.

Papa did have friends who were girls, like Rica, who also immigrated to America, but the priesthood was on his mind and he didn't want to get involved with a girl. When Papa would be working up the slope of the mountain and he would see Rica below in her family's farm, he would yodel a specific yodel to her and she had a specific yodel response for him.

At age twenty-eight, Papa would meet a girl who would capture his heart. Papa had been in the United States for about seven years when my mother's family immigrated to the United States for the second time. They had immigrated here to the coal mining town of Hazelton, Pennsylvania, the first time but returned to the old country for an extended visit. While they were there the borders were shut due to the First World War. About nine years after the war ended, they decided to come to

America permanently. This time they chose to join family and friends in Melrose Park, Illinois.

Just before leaving for America, my mother's parents left to travel to a distant city to say goodbye to two of their sons, Silvio and Victor, who were in the seminary studying for the priesthood. My mother, who had just turned twenty, was left to finish the packing, then take the younger children and the family belongings on the train to meet her parents at a designated place where they would board the ship for America. As she was doing so, Papa's father sent her a message saying he wanted to see her before she left.

Mama went to the Rauzi home. My grandfather, Archangelo, gave her his gold and onyx ring, telling her that he wanted her to deliver it to his son, Joseph. He specifically wanted her to deliver it to him. It was never said, but is commonly believed, that he wanted Papa to meet this pretty and very good girl. Because Papa was twenty-eight, we think our grandfather thought it was time for him to marry. He cautioned my mother to keep the ring in a careful place so as not to lose it. She was really offended at this. As she said, "Here I was, twenty, and left to finish the packing and take care of my young brothers and sister and he thinks I'm not responsible!" In his senior years, Papa passed the ring on to our oldest brother, Archie (Archangelo) who in turn passed it on to his oldest son, Joseph.

It just so happened that when my mother's family arrived in Melrose Park in the spring of 1928, they moved into a flat right next door to where my father and his friends lived. Mama delivered the ring. As Papa said, "I never thought about marriage until I saw your mama." They were married four months after they first met. That romance lasted sixty-three years. Mama and Papa fell in love immediately and forever.

Living next door to Papa was a bonus for Mama. She said that she and her sister Frieda used to watch Papa coming and going next door from their second floor bedroom window and giggle. Papa, however, had competitors. Several men from Cloz started visiting Mama. Papa asked for permission to do so also.

Mama, on the left, and her sister, Frieda.

On one occasion, he was upstairs visiting with her when another suitor came to the house. He asked for Mama and my grandmother told him she was busy upstairs. He kept insisting and finally brushed past my grandmother. Going upstairs and finding my father with her, he raised a ruckus and was furious with my grandmother. He was quite nasty about it. Mama was always shy in talking about it, but evidently she had quite a few fellows in Cloz and in the U.S. interested in her.

Mama and Papa went on one unchaperoned date before they were married. Papa borrowed a car and drove her to a jeweler to buy their wedding rings. At one point they crossed the long Mannheim bridge over what was and still is one of the largest railroad switching yards in the United States. They had stopped to buy ice cream cones before going to the jeweler. Through the years we would at times cross that bridge with one or both of my parents in the car and my mother would always remember their date and say, "Papa bought me a big ice cream cone and I couldn't finish it." While the comment doesn't seem very romantic, the fact that she always remembered the events of their "date" is.

At this point I should add that my mother had been my grandmother's main helper. She saw clearly the tremendous struggles her mother had to endure and vowed she would never marry, that she would always stay home to take care of her mother. But Papa stole her heart. Her mother was in her late forties and was very arthritic with serious debilitating back pain. Mama pleaded with her younger sister Frieda, asking her not to enter the convent as she intended, that she would stay home to help their mother. Frieda promised to do so, but her desire to be a nun was too great and she left for the convent shortly after Mama and Papa were married. Despite being married, Mama continued to take care of her mother, and did so for the rest of her mom's life.

As I mentioned, they were married four months after they met. It was Papa's intention to get married quietly. He didn't want a big fuss, and Mama's mother was in the hospital. Papa made all the arrangements. He prepared a flat for them to live in. He hired some ladies to cook a special meal at this flat when the wedding party and family members came home from the church. Then he said he bought a very, very expensive black silk suit for this most important event in his life.

Mama wore a cream-colored dress with a drop waist of silk chiffon which came to mid-calf length, and a cream-colored cloche hat. This was high style in 1928. She wanted to wear a long white dress and veil which was just coming into fashion, but my father asked her not to. He thought it was not dignified, and pretentious. When they sent their wedding pictures to

Papa's parents, his father wrote back saying that the photographs were nice and that Mama was lovely, but that Papa could cut off some of his pant legs to cover her legs. Women in Cloz were still wearing dresses to their ankles and up to their necks. Mama's legs showing must have been a difficult adjustment for them.

Word got out that Papa was to be married on August 15th at a private wedding. Papa had been a very involved person in the church and community, and a most desirable, handsome, eligible bachelor in Melrose Park for seven years.

Even back in Cloz, one woman who still hoped for Papa's love, lied to his parents saying that she heard Mama was a very sickly woman. She hoped to prevent the marriage and that Papa might return to Cloz to marry her some day. Women in Melrose Park had the same hope. Papa's parents wrote to voice their concern about Mama's health, and Papa responded that even if she were deathly ill he would still marry her. Years later, when Mama returned to Cloz for a visit, she met this woman on a stairwell. The lady tearfully apologized for her actions. Mama didn't have good feelings toward the woman for what she had done, but was glad she apologized.

People in Melrose Park who were close to Papa told him that even if it was a private wedding and they weren't invited, they were coming to the wedding anyway. Others questioned why the wedding was so quick and being kept small and quiet. Was something wrong? They hinted at scandal. Others were just curious to see who this girl was who finally captured Joseph!

So their wedding became a big event. On that day, my father picked up my mother, her father, and sister Frieda who was the maid of honor, and then drove to the hospital to pick up my grandmother at the hospital where she was a patient, arriving at Our Lady of Mount Carmel Church to find the church packed.

Mama and Papa on their wedding day, August 15, 1928.

Papa then realized that his friends meant what they said. He quickly requested special permission from Father Franch to use the school hall for a reception, which was not done in those days. He sent his soon-to-be brothers-in-law to a nearby store to buy sandwich meats, Italian bread, pop, beer, etc., for a quickly laid-out reception lunch. "All these people came, filling the hall! They came with gifts," Papa said. Mama was hugged and kissed by so many well wishers that she got sick to her stomach. Papa had to make her tea to calm her upset stomach on their wedding night.

The last thing Papa told me of their wedding was that his friends tied pots and pans to the springs under their bed. When they got into bed the pans created a lot of clanging, banging noise. He laughed when telling me that.

They were married on August 15, 1928.

CHAPTER 6

1929 DEPRESSION, FAMILY AND LIVING CONDITIONS

Fourteen months after they were married, the Great Depression of 1929 happened. Having come from poorer lives in the old country, Mama and Papa knew how to live sparingly, but despite that, the rationing of cooking supplies and durable goods was hard on them. Blessedly, Papa didn't lose his job during those trying times because the cemetery was busy as the tragedies of the Depression continued. Those years and the Second World War that followed not too many years later were years of fantastic events in Papa's life, as well as years of great effort to support a family of seven children.

Four months before the Stock Market Crash, Mama gave birth to their first child, a son, Archie (Archangelo). Candido (Dominic), Miriam, Lino, George and Sylvia all followed every year-and-a-half or two. Francis (Frank), the last child, followed six years later. It wasn't long before they

Papa stands in the yard of the three-flat home.

outgrew their flat and had to rent a home on 18th Avenue in Melrose Park, about a mile or so from Mama's parents. Daily, Mama did her housework, baked the day's bread for her family and for her parents' family. She then bundled up the children, always a baby in a buggy, and walked to my grandparents' home to bring the bread and do the housework for her mother.

Eventually, her mother insisted on buying a large three-flat home with some inheritance money she had so that Mama wouldn't have to make that daily trip. My grandparents lived in the English basement flat, we lived in the middle flat, and Uncle Joe and Aunt Catherine lived upstairs with our cousins Josephine and Michael.

At this point I need to tell you about Mama's parents because our grandmother's presence in Mama and Papa's home greatly affected Papa's life. We called our grandfather Noni (instead of Nono, which means grandfather in Italian). He was Joseph Zanoni, a carpenter and home builder; a quiet, kindly natured, good man. Nona (Italian for grandmother) was Florence Luchi Zanoni, a woman totally focused on what was good for her family, with great love – an extremely intelligent woman with an inborn dignity about her and excellent natural business sense.

Nona came to the United States the first time as a very little girl, in about 1886. Her parents moved from Cloz, Austria, to Hazelton, Pennsylvania, so her father could work in the coal mines. Her first years of school were in America, so she spoke perfect English all her life.

When a preteen, her family returned to Cloz where her father started a brick-making business. There, she completed her basic education, ending at age fourteen. Upon her graduation, her teacher and the parish priest begged Nona's father, Stefano Luchi, to allow her to go on to college because of her exceptional intelligence. He refused, telling them that since their only son died as an infant, she was their only child and was needed to help with the brick-making business. Besides her intelligence, as yet a young teenager, her sewing and embroidery abilities were superior. She taught others, and at times sewed for them.

My grandmother and her parents

Also, as I mentioned, Nona had an inborn dignity about her which must have come from her maternal ancestry. Her great-grandparents on her mother's side were a Marquis and Marquise who were granted their titles because of their generosity and humanitarian work for their fellow countrymen. Nona grew up with the family's Coat of Arms over the doorway of their home. Our family is still tracing that part of our family history.

Nona and Noni were married in January 1902. Their first child, a son, Albino, was born in the spring of 1903 and died six months later of dysentery. Also in their first years of marriage, Nona taught Noni to speak English. She then sent him ahead to the United States to find work and prepare a place for them. Nona's father, Stefano, died in 1904, so Nona took her mother with her and her infant son Serafino to join her husband who was now a unionized carpenter in Hazelton, Pennsylvania. She and her mother did not, however, sell their property and farm in Cloz.

Once settled in Hazelton, Nona immediately saw a business opportunity to open a small store near the schools that sold school supplies and ice cream. There wasn't any store like that near the schools. It would be an easy business to manage. Noni, however, was a creative person, a builder, but not a businessman and afraid of the money risk. He refused to allow her to open her store. At that time, a husband's permission and signature were required. Her cousin picked up the idea from her and became quite wealthy.

Noni did, however, allow Nona to take borders, who were all workers in the mine, into their large home. She had to hand-scrub their filthy mining clothes, clean their rooms, cook large meals and pack large lunches for them. She also gave birth to four more children during those years. One day she served dinner as usual to a large table full of these men and then quietly went upstairs to deliver her baby. When the men heard the baby had been born, they bought a quarter-barrel of beer and celebrated into the night.

Eventually, they returned to Cloz in 1913 because Noni's brother was killed while trying to rescue miners after an explosion in the mine. Noni felt it was his responsibility to escort his widowed sister-in-law and her baby back to Cloz. He also wanted to go home for a long visit. They sold their home and Nona had to pack all their belongings for their return to Cloz. The ocean voyage happened as winter was approaching and Nona had a baby in arms, plus her four other small children.

The political climate was becoming very strained between Austria and Italy, and Nona kept urging Noni to return to America because she was sure a war was soon to erupt, but Noni disagreed. On July 28, 1914, the First World War began. The Austrian borders were closed and, at age forty, Noni was drafted into the army despite his American citizenship. Through a clever ruse, he managed to get himself assigned to army hospital work and didn't have to go into battle.

In Cloz, they lived in the home and small farm owned by Nona's mother, who died there five years later in 1919. Nona now had to leave her babies in the care of my mother, her oldest daughter Paolina, who was then only a young child, and also Felicita, a teenage relative, so she could work the farm. She also opened a small shop where she sold copper household necessities. During those war years, she lost another child, Dolores, in her infancy, also due to dysentery. She mourned her two babies until the day she died, keeping their pictures on her dresser all her life. Between 1915 and 1922, she gave birth to the last of her children, three sons.

It was not only difficult for her to do the farming, but the inequality of the irrigation route from the mountaintop to farmers below made it harder. The farmers with higher farm plots got a better water supply. She collected signatures from the other farmers on a petition demanding an irrigation route that would benefit all the farmers. Having won this cause, she then went out with the men and helped build that irrigation system. Years later, in the United States, she was talking about her efforts to get the irrigation system changed and built with some old men from Cloz who had also immigrated to Melrose Park and who remembered the situation. But they gave Nona no credit. They even laughed at her, saying, "Yah, Florence, you're only a woman. How can you say you did that!"

I remember her telling me all these stories, which are just a few in the long history of her life. There was no mistaking the irritation and indignation in her voice. She resented the dominance, lack of respect and lack of good business sense of the men in her life. You can't blame her; it was quite understandable and an honest reaction. She suffered a great deal under their control.

In very early spring of 1928, they finally returned to the

United States. Nona eventually set two of her older sons up in a grocery business in Melrose Park and saw to it that their son Bonfiglio received his medical degree as a podiatrist. She was also always aware of good business opportunities or property of quality. At one point, she saw a well-built, large brick home which she wanted to buy. Having gone through hard times in Cloz, then the war and the Depression in the United States, Noni was reluctant to take on a mortgage, even though the price of the home was very good. He refused to buy it. Nona pointed to that house many times over the years. She hated missing out on a good opportunity that would benefit her family.

Finally, in 1939, she was able to enjoy the satisfaction of making a purchase that indeed has benefitted her family ever since. On Labor Day, Nona and some of the family took a trip to Norway, Michigan, to see where her father had worked in the mines from 1870 to 1875. He had walked, following the railroad lines, from Hazelton, Pennsylvania, to do so, and now Nona was retracing his steps. She was also determined to find a lost cousin in that town. Her mother's sister had died there in childbirth and the family never again heard of the baby. Nona searched, investigated, and eventually found him. He was a wonderful man and they became dear friends.

There in the Norway, Vulcan area, Nona saw beautiful country that in many ways resembled the old country. She also saw that it would be a wonderful place for her family to spend the summers. She returned the following year and this time she did buy a home she wanted. It was a cottage on the Hamilton Lakes in Vulcan. Noni enlarged the cottage so that there were dormitory-style, large bedrooms for their children and grandchildren. After the Second World War, their son Joseph bought a large piece of land also on the lake and built a summer resort which is still in operation today.

Later, she bought an old house in the town of Norway

The family picture of Nona and Noni.

because she felt her arthritis worsen being so close to the humidity of the lake. Being married to a carpenter and very intelligent, she saw to it that the house was properly fixed up, remodeling it to accommodate a larger and up-to-date kitchen. I can remember that whenever Nona had to walk up or down a set of stairs that were not properly given the correct rise or width of stair, she would tap the stairs with her cane and say, "These stairs are not made right." I remember also that she greatly admired my husband because he took the time to take apart her favorite chair which was becoming very wobbly, and then he carefully put it back together with glue and reinforcements, giving her back a sturdy chair. He had done it right, and she loved him for it.

You most likely are wondering what all this has to do with Papa. Well, Nona had a long history of frustration with the men who controlled her life, well-intentioned though their decisions were. They were made by men who loved her but who made bad decisions regarding her needs, her future, and her wise insights, all of which made her life very difficult. She had to struggle and work hard where she could have been fulfilled in life, educated, comfortable and even affluent had she not been so restricted. As a result, Nona, though devoted to her sons and family, lost her patience and tolerance of men in general and their power over her good sense.

All this spilled over into her protectiveness over her daughter and irritation with her son-in-law, my parents. When they first arrived in Melrose Park, Mama went to work in a factory with her friends. She came home her first day on the job all covered in factory dirt. Nona became upset and said that her daughter would never work in that condition again. Mama never held a job outside the home from that day on. Then, after my parents married, Nona saw her as a very busy mother constantly working while Papa was at work and at a lot of evening meetings at church all the time. She was not very pleased with Papa.

Nona and Noni lived with my parents and our family until they died and were very much a part of Papa's life. However, Nona was outspoken when she didn't like what she saw or didn't agree with. It was difficult at times and caused tension also between my parents, but for sure my grandparents were cared for lovingly. I never heard Papa speak disrespectfully to Nona or about Nona, and he seemed to have an understanding and compassion for her struggles in life. He saw her goodness but, still, her comments often had him walking away mumbling to himself.

In her last years, Nona was pretty much confined to her bed. I remember her praying for her family constantly during those years. Then Mama became ill with heart problems. For a long while, Papa took care of both of them, cooking, cleaning, bringing them their food and medicine and Holy Communion after he went to daily morning Mass. He even emptied Nona's bedside commode. All this, while still working next door at his job at the church. Nona died in 1975 at the age of ninety-four and Papa was in his seventies. It was only the second time I ever saw Papa cry.

It is important to note here that in those days it was quite common for grandparents to live with their children and they were very much part of the family. Most of the Italian grandparents I knew were often unafraid of speaking their minds in family situations. Everyone thought they had a right to do so, and grandparents certainly did.

Now getting back to the three-flat where we lived for about fourteen years with Nona, Noni, Uncle Joe, Aunt Catherine and

Mama and Papa and son, Frank, in the yard, with the grape arbor behind them.

cousins. The house had a big side yard and a small backyard, and a bench swing that was suspended from a frame with a grape arbor over it that came up the back and over the top of the frame and swing, as well as the left and right sides. There was a garden in the small backyard, a gazebo in the side yard which no one seemed to use, a large garage back by the alley, and a big doghouse for Snoopy, our Water Spaniel dog. There was a little flower garden along the side of the house near Nona and Noni's door.

In front there were three cement steps that led up to a cement landing, then about twelve wooden steps that led up to a small wooden entrance porch to our second floor flat. The cement landing, wooden steps and small porch were wrapped in lattice woodwork. The third floor, and actually all three floors, could be reached by the back entrance. A marvelous bannister led from the second to the third floor. We kids thought it was the greatest ride when we slid down that bannister.

As I describe our home, it brings to mind that the best part of our years was that there were a lot of relatives and friends, a lot of kids to play with. On our long block there were one hundred children. I counted them one day. Our families no longer own that house.

As more children were born, our flat became very crowded but we kids didn't know it. We were just enjoying life. Mama, however, had to have enormous patience. When the weather didn't permit her to hang clothes from the clothesline pulley which was attached to the back porch window and across the yard to the roof of the garage, she had to hang the wet laundry on lines stretched across our large kitchen. We kids had great fun running through the rows of damp clothes. Mama washed the clothes in a wringer washing machine in our oversized bathroom and rinsed them in the bathtub. The water heater was also housed in the bathroom.

My parents' bedroom had a crib in it for many years, and the one other bedroom was shared by my five brothers, sleeping two and three in a bed. My sister and I slept on couches in the front entrance hallway. There was a small livingroom at the front of the house which was hardly ever used, as most of the visiting happened around the kitchen table. Off the kitchen was a long walk-in pantry with cabinets and counters on both sides.

On a high shelf in the pantry, just inside the door, sat a 1930s radio. We kids would lie on the kitchen floor after school listening to the fifteen-minute serial programs such as *Captain Midnight, Dick Tracy, Terry and the Pirates, The Lone Ranger*, etc. Our mother would have to step over our bodies as she went in and out of the pantry while cooking dinner. On Saturday nights when we children had already gone to bed, our parents and relatives would sit around the kitchen table having coffee and sweets while listening to an adult cowboy series called *Avanti Cimonelo*.

Perishable food was kept in our wooden icebox until Mama and Papa could afford a refrigerator. But, oh, that icebox was a great source of adventure and fun for us children. The iceman came regularly in a big truck. He knew what size block of ice his customers used; a twenty-five-cent or fifty-cent size. He would split off that size with his icepick and then hoist it on his shoulder, which was protected by a large piece of leather, holding the ice with rounded tongs.

When he was inside the houses, we children scrambled up onto the truck picking up the small pieces of chipped-off ice to suck on. I was usually the look-out. My job was to warn the kids when the iceman was leaving the house. Some of the boys would pull the pick out of the wall where the iceman had stuck it, and would chip off some chunks of ice if not enough were found on the floor. I think the iceman always knew what we were up to and I also think he purposely left us a good supply of ice chips.

Mama cooked our dinners on a black combination gas burner and wood and coal-burning stove. She would remove the rings of metal from the top of the wood-burning side and set the very thick copper kettle they brought from Cloz right down on the flames to cook the polenta. At times, Papa would cook Sunday dinner for Mama. We usually had beef, gravy and mashed potatoes on Sunday, and Dominic always mashed the potatoes with a hand masher.

Papa also helped Mama in other ways. His days started very early. He got up, ate his pane e' café (bread and coffee) or potate rostede. Then he would mop the kitchen floor for my mother because there were always babies crawling around as they tried to learn to walk. Next he biked about six blocks to the bakery to buy day-old bread, which was cheaper. There were too many of us for Mama to continue all that baking.

This done, he then biked nine miles to work at the cemetery. When milk was needed, Papa and one of the men who had a car would stop at a farm close to the cemetery to buy milk, bringing it home in tall, metal milk cans that you now see in antique stores or are used as umbrella stands and porch decorations. It was a great challenge for us kids to sneak a spoon of cream off the top before we were caught – a simple joy during poorer years.

The Depression and World War II years were hard for almost everyone. People didn't waste anything and learned how to make do with what they had. Papa learned to repair our shoes. He had a metal shoe repair stand with metal foot forms so he could repair any size shoe. Tracing the sole of the shoe on a thick piece of tan-colored leather, he then cut out the new sole with a hooked blade knife and nailed it to the bottoms of the shoes. As we grew, our shoes were passed down to the next child. At one point, I had to wear my brother's shoes for a couple of weeks until my parents could manage the money for a pair of girl's shoes.

Despite all their frugality there was a time when my parents had less than fifty cents and many days before payday. That week there were a lot of burials at the cemetery and my father was asked to work on Sunday. Because of Papa's firm belief that you never work on Sunday unless it's to help someone in great need, he refused and repeatedly told his boss he wouldn't work. Sunday was for God and family, not for making money. That Sunday he was really torn between his faithfulness to God and his obligation to earn money for his family.

While standing in front of the church after Mass on Sunday and feeling very downhearted about the situation, a friend came up to Papa and firmly shook his hand, saying, "Joe, I want to thank you for what you did for me." Papa was bewildered and said that he never was able to remember what he had done for the man. Before he could say anything, the man walked away. It was then that Papa felt the twenty dollar bill in his hand. At that time, twenty dollars was an enormous amount of money. Papa honored God and God provided for him.

Beyond the need to have enough money to buy food and pay expenses in those lean years, the immigrants also continued to provide for other needs just as they had done in the old country all their lives – having a good vegetable garden, growing fruit trees, and making wine and whiskey. The United States, however, had enacted a law prohibiting the making and selling of liquor – the law we all know as "Prohibition." The European people always made their own wine and whiskey, continuing to do so in America, helping each other with this yearly job. They passed their copper stills around from family to family. The wine and whiskey weren't sold; it was strictly for home use.

Nevertheless, every once in a while one of them would be hauled off to jail. Papa was pretty much the spokesman for his fellow immigrants. He would have to go to the police station and argue them out of trouble with the authorities. One bitter, cold night there was a large house fire next to where my parents lived. Papa opened their home to the firemen and policemen who would take turns coming in to warm up and have some coffee. Papa would offer them some homemade whiskey (called grappa) in their coffee to help warm them up, and they all gladly accepted. When the fire was extinguished and the Police Chief was leaving, Papa said to him, "You drank our whiskey with us, so now we don't expect any more trouble." No more arrests were made. That settled the situation.

Also, out of the need to conserve money, Papa learned how to cut hair. He cut hair for all the men and boys – his sons, our grandfather, uncles, cousins, and some friends. In her last years, Mama remembered Papa's barbering enthusiasm with horror because as he was giving all my brothers their summer crewcuts, he decided that a crewcut would also be cooler for our sister Miriam, then a cute little four-year-old. A big mistake!

He kept cutting hair for family until his late seventies. The guys knew that if they wiggled too much, they could expect a good tap on the top of the head with the comb and the reprimand, "stai fermo," which meant "stay still." We all had a good laugh when Papa was in his eighties and my brother Dominic was cutting his hair. Papa kept turning his head to talk with Mama. My brother tapped him on the head with the comb and demanded playfully, stai fermo!

There was one more necessity in Mama's life in those early years of their marriage and she took care of it wisely and cleverly. As children continued to be born, Papa still remained very involved with many evening meetings at the church and just generally helping Father Franch as he had done for many years before. On Sunday, he ushered and helped out at all the Masses. Mama's patience finally gave out. When he arrived home one night from yet another meeting, he found his suitcase packed at the back kitchen door. Mama said calmly, "You spend so much time over at the church rectory that I thought it would be easier for you if you just took your clothes and stayed there." Needless to say, he took her action very much to heart and he modified his commitments.

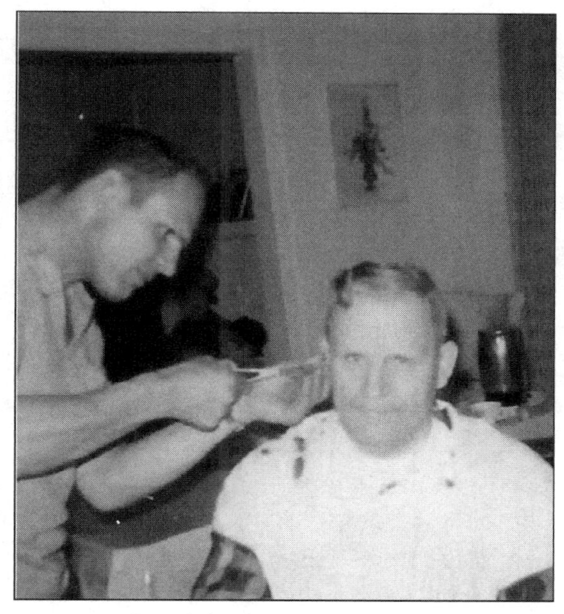

Dominic gives Papa a haircut

He was gone, however, every weekday evening during November when he took on some short-term work to earn a little extra money, and he continued doing that until the early 1950s. He worked at Rizzi Florist. Caesar Rizzi was a "piasano" (friend) from Cloz. In November, they made pine bough grave coverings for Christmas. Mount Carmel Cemetery was located across the street.

Caesar had a son, Eddie, who was the same age as Bunnie, a girl who worked in the office. Papa saw that they were both good young people and thought they made a good match, so he encouraged their relationship. Eddie and Bunnie did get married and remained very close to Papa and Mama all their lives. I never knew of another instance where Papa played matchmaker. He was not one to interfere with other people's lives.

There was one time, however, when Papa purposely tried to

help a friend appreciate life. For the sake of privacy, I've changed the man's name to Jack. Jack was a good man, involved in a lot of organizations, but people were getting fed up with him because he complained incessantly. His wife and children were miserable because nothing was ever good enough or right as far as Jack was concerned. One day my father stopped at his house and, speaking to both Jack and his wife, he made an appointment to take Jack somewhere on Sunday but he wouldn't tell them where.

On Sunday, Papa picked him up and took him to Hines Veterans Hospital, in Maywood, Illinois. Papa volunteered there in wards where the public was not allowed. The war casualties were atrocious. Men with no arms and legs lay in basket-like beds. Body parts of other soldiers were mutilated. Papa would visit these men and write letters in Italian for them. He got permission to allow Jack to accompany him that Sunday. After the visit, Jack was visibly shaken and said absolutely nothing, silent all the way home. He never complained about anything again. His wife begged Papa, "What did you do to my husband? Where did you take him?"

Papa allowed Jack the privacy of telling her himself when he was ready. Papa never told anyone what caused Jack to have a new grateful attitude and happier life. Because Jack has been dead for many years, Papa felt okay in telling me.

CHAPTER 7

CEMETERY JOB

In those early years of the twenties, thirties, and forties, Papa continued working at Mount Carmel Cemetery. He would delightfully scare us with his interesting accounts of things that happened at the cemetery. Here are some of his stories.

First of all, as I mentioned before, he was repeatedly asked to be a foreman but didn't want to be a boss. His work ethic and leadership always put him in interesting situations, however, such as overseeing the job of moving Al Capone's grave. Al Capone had initially been buried in an undisclosed place after his death. He was now being buried in a high security grave with poured cement and a large headstone. Bushes in front of the stone partially covered the name so that people still didn't really see it. In the 1980s, my brother George called Papa from his home in Minnesota, telling Papa that he was on television. "But what you talking about?" Papa questioned. It was a documentary on Al Capone and there was Papa in his denim coveralls and long workman's denim jacket directing the handling of the casket.

He also talked of the burial of another gangster. There were twenty-six funeral cars of flowers. Papa had never seen so many flowers at one funeral. Several days later he had to go into the cooler where bodies are kept while awaiting burial. Conditions were difficult in the United States and there were a lot of deaths, more than could be buried immediately, so the caskets had to be stored in a cooler until burial. "I went in," Papa said, "and I had my clipboard, you know, with the names on it. I was backing down the row while I was checking for the name I wanted. There were caskets on both sides. All of a sudden I feel icy cold fingers; they grab me by the neck and shoulder. I froze. I waited for over a minute and the hands don't move, so I decided it's better to see who or what was attacking me. I jumped forward and turned around in the same time so I could face him. It was a life-sized body of the gangster all made out of flowers and the hands made of wax. I backed into the hands

Papa in his later years, at work at the Mount Carmel Cemetery.

and they were cold from the cooler."

"One time," Papa said, "we had to move a body of a little baby girl about one-year-old to a spot where her family bought a family plot. I was on the bottom, standing in the grave, working the straps around the coffin, and the other guy was up above to work the machine to pull it up. All of a sudden the straps fall on my head and I look up. The guy was gone. I climb up to see him running away so I call him back to see what's wrong. He tell me that the baby was crying in the coffin. After a while I convince him that this is not possible, she is dead over a year. Again I prepare the straps and we start to lift the coffin. Again the straps fall on my head. This time the other guy is really scared, so we get the foreman and we get permission to open the casket. In with the baby was a big doll, and every time we move the casket the doll said, 'Mama.'"

There were no fences that kept people out of the cemetery in those early years. One hot summer day, Papa was working way into the night. He heard screams in one of the sections. Papa drove his truck quietly and without lights on, getting as close as possible, then turned off his motor. He first saw a car parked in the dark, but then was greatly relieved to see parents tending to a grave while their screaming children were running through the water of the cemetery faucet used for watering.

Papa said he watched much graveside grief, but one sight he never forgot. A woman became hysterical as the casket was lowered into the grave and she tried to throw herself in the grave with it. When restrained, she screamed that she wouldn't leave the grave. Lunging herself to the ground, she clamped her mouth around a thorny rosebush branch near the gravesite.

On another occasion, Papa was told to clear the area of people around the section where one of the more notorious gangsters was buried. Shortly later, a long black car drove into the section and a woman dressed all in black emerged from the back seat. She stood in front of the grave for a while and then she left. Papa remembers it vividly because as he watched her he saw such a coldness about her demeanor. He repeated the word "cold" several times while shaking his head with a frown on his face. Then he said, "I never in my life saw such a cold woman."

There was also good-natured fun among the men who worked at the cemetery. Papa was quite pleased that when they would compete to see who could lift heavy objects single-handed, no one was able to lift more than he did. He also laughed at how one big, husky guy kept everyone mystified for a long time by telling them he only ate one sandwich at lunchtime. He was really a big fellow. The men didn't have a lunchroom so they would eat while sitting with their backs against a tree. One day, Papa passed by as this man took out his lunch. It was only one sandwich – a full length loaf of french bread, sliced lengthwise and filled with sandwich meats.

As I mentioned, the men didn't have a warm, comfortable place to go to eat their lunches. Other working conditions also weren't good, and the wages were not as good as they should have been and they didn't have any benefits. The cemetery board of the Chicago Catholic Diocese was unaware of conditions but were looking into the matter because it had become an issue. Papa had been working at the cemetery for about twenty-six years when all this came about. The administrators of the cemetery told Papa that because they knew he was a just man who would present the problems in a truthful and understanding manner, they wanted him to represent the workers at a meeting at the Diocese office in Chicago.

Dressed in his Sunday suit, Papa sat in the Chicago office and forthrightly presented the situation. As a result of his presentation of the facts, working conditions were greatly improved, wages increased, and a lunchroom was provided. A pension was also set in place, as well as other benefits. "I just told them the way things are," Papa said, matter-of-factly. The Catholic Diocese was grateful to him.

Unfortunately, before the benefits could be implemented, the harsh conditions had taken their toll on Papa. He ended up in the hospital with severe sciatica for several months. He had to quit the cemetery work he loved so much and was never able to receive the benefits he won for cemetery workers. When able to return to work, Papa worked in a local factory for a while and then as a janitor at Our Lady of Mount Carmel Church and school.

CHAPTER 8

FEAST OF OUR LADY OF MOUNT CARMEL, RETURN TO CLOZ

The Feast of Our Lady of Mount Carmel was the most important day of the year for my father. Thousands of people came from all over Chicago and suburbs, and from out-of-state as well. It was and still is (for over one hundred years) a week-long festivity culminating on Sunday with a Mass celebrated outdoors to accommodate the large number of people attending. This was followed by a procession through three miles of the town. Families decorated their front porches with fancy linens, flowers, candles, and statues of Jesus and the Blessed Virgin.

Papa was always found in front of Our Lady's statue.

Family members came home from out-of-state for their vacation during the Feast because families reunited at that time. Tables, chairs, and a lot of special food were seen in every yard. The families of the entire town celebrated the event they had waited for all year.

It is a special and joyful time. Hundreds of people march, constantly singing and praying in the procession. Many wear various uniforms of different religious societies they belong to. They carry flowers, banners, candle houses, and statues. The village band marches, playing hymns and, most importantly, the men of the Holy Name of Jesus Society carry the large statue of Our Lady of Mount Carmel.

For fifty years, Papa was the only one who would climb up a ladder and remove the statue of the Blessed Mother from a glass case where it is kept on a high ledge near the altar. He then returned the statue when it arrived back into the church after the procession. During the Mass and the procession Papa was where the Blessed Mother's statue was.

He was also one of the main people on the Feast Committee. Father Franch formed the committee in 1932 with twelve men who he referred to as the "twelve apostles." Papa had also been deputized as a special policeman with uniform, badge, and gun for security needs for large religious gatherings. He served in this capacity at the World Eucharistic Congress at Soldier Field in Chicago in 1926.

Papa was deputized for security needs at large religious gatherings.

Numerous donations were made at the church, which helped this immigrant parish. Father Franch knew it wouldn't be safe to keep such a large amount of money in the rectory, so he asked

Paul Abate, who owned a currency exchange business, to transfer the money to his business safe because the banks were closed. Papa was to accompany Paul in the capacity of Special Police.

As they were leaving the front door of the rectory with the money bags, gunshots were directed at them. One bullet just missed my father and lodged in a nearby tree. Paul and Papa made it to the car and began to drive fast with Paul at the wheel. They were being pursued at high speed while being shot at. "Shoot, Joe, shoot," Paul yelled at Papa, who then began returning the gunfire. At one point, Paul drove up a sidewalk, eventually turning down some alleys to lose the other car, which they finally did. Then he and Papa ran into a basement apartment of someone they knew, staying there a long while until it was safe to leave.

During this week-long feast, people gathered at Church each evening to attend a special prayer service called a novena, and they then would spend some time enjoying the festivities and food at the various stands set up around the church property.

On one occasion during the feast there was a problem, which eventually brought in a Mafia figure. Food stands and other stands were erected, as I said, on and around the church property. To help defray costs and help with the parish's yearly budget, a small fee was asked of the vendors to rent the space. One of the vendors either refused to pay the fee when my father approached them or at times would give him small change as a partial payment. When Papa lost his patience with them, they threatened that they had Mafia friends and that Papa had better leave them alone.

The following day, a local man and a well-known Mafia member approached my father with his two henchmen at either side. He said, "Joe, I hear you're bothering my friends at the stand across the street. You better leave them alone.

Understand?" Papa was furious and replied, "I knew you when you were just a little kid and here you are now denying the church the little money it needs, money given to honor the Blessed Mother! If your mother was alive, she would be ashamed and she would slap you in the face." With that, he turned his back on the man and walked away.

His friends begged, "Joe, do you know who you were taking to? Be careful." "I knew him when he was a kid. I'm not afraid of him," Papa snapped back at them. He then immediately went over to the vendor's stand and grabbed the two-by-four wood which was holding up the stand's front section and began shaking it and the whole stand fiercely, saying, "Give me all that you owe right now or I'll pull the whole stand down." They paid up and there was no more trouble.

On another occasion, the Mafia began extorting protection money from the vendors, threatening to cut off their electricity if they didn't pay up. These gangsters, for some reason, would come into Melrose Park via the Lake Street electric streetcar and walk the few blocks to the church area. Papa gathered a group of the Feast workers and posted them on the three corners of the intersecting street by the church, and he stood on the fourth corner. When he saw the two men coming, Papa gave the signal. All the workers posted on the corners and Papa converged on the men and surrounded them. Papa told them, "Turn around and head back up to Lake Street." They did, with Papa and the others right behind them. When the next streetcar came along, Papa told them that if they knew what was good for them they better not return – and they didn't.

Now don't get the impression that the Feast of Our Lady of Mount Carmel, which has been happening for over a hundred years, is a raucous affair. These incidents were just a sign of the times and isolated. The Feast is a time of great devotion and love for the Blessed Mother. Papa deeply loved her and the work he did in her honor was very important to him from the time he arrived in Melrose Park in his young twenties until his late seventies when he began staying in Michigan for the summer with my mother and grandmother.

Every July, in Michigan, when the Feast was taking place in Melrose Park, Papa would be very quiet all day and constantly praying his rosary. At times I saw tears welling in his eyes. Now he was far away in Michigan and sad on that day.

In the late thirties, another series of interesting events happened in Papa's life surrounding a trip back to Cloz to visit his parents and family. Papa was about thirty-seven and this was his first and only trip back to Cloz. He was reluctant to go but my mother insisted that he needed to go right away. Papa's mother wasn't well and there was a threat of war. Mama urged Papa to go, telling him that if he didn't and a war broke out, he might never see his mother alive again.

Italian citizens are Italian citizens for life, even if they become citizens of another country. If they were in Italy for a visit in those days and a war started, they could very well be pressed into military service regardless of their citizenship elsewhere. My father's images of starvation, hardship, and brutal war during the First World War caused him not to want to risk being caught there and forced back into the military, so he devised a plan. First, he went to the Italian Consulate in Chicago. He knew him personally from the dinners he served while the Consul visited Father Franch at Mount Carmel Parish. Papa received a letter of free passage and a recommendation from him. He then went to the Consuls of all the border countries that immediately surrounded Austria and Northern Italy and received free passage signatures from all of them as well. He figured that if war did erupt, he had a fair chance of getting out of the country and back to his family in the United States.

Getting off the ship in Italy, he then had to board a train to

Papa, an imposing gentleman in his full-length coat
which was lined with gold coins.

travel to Rome where he was to stay at a monastery for the night. The trains at that time had seating compartments that seated four people. Papa entered his compartment to find that it was also being occupied by one of Mussolini's officers. Trying not to show fear, Papa casually entered. Before sitting down he had another dilemma, however. It was against the law to bring a great deal of money into Italy, especially gold.

Many immigrant friends in Melrose Park had pressed Papa to please bring their money home to their families in Cloz. It added up to quite a bit of money, which had been changed into gold coins. His mother-in-law, Nona, was an accomplished seamstress. She opened up the lining of his heavy, full-length, fur-trimmed coat and sewed the gold coins into its lining in individual pockets so they wouldn't clank together. Here he now was with a coat full of gold facing this Italian officer. Keeping up his casual manner, he took off his coat before sitting and flung it over the seat carelessly.

The two men acknowledged each other. The officer then went back to reading his paper and smoking his cigar. Papa picked up a newspaper and busied himself reading, looking out the window, and smoking his cigarettes. On occasion, he would steal a look at the officer, only to find the officer looking at him. Not wanting to tangle with him, Papa didn't start any conversation and planned a way to dodge the officer when they got off the train.

When they arrived at Rome, Papa left quickly and took what he thought was an elusive way out to the main exit. When he got there, the officer was standing at the exit. He asked Papa where he was going to be staying since it was close to midnight. Papa told him he had arrangements to stay at the monastery. The officer insisted that it was much too late to try to locate the monastery and invited my father to stay at his hotel, explaining that all the officers were in Rome for a parade honoring

Mussolini the following day. Papa was trapped. He couldn't refuse the officer without raising suspicion. He had to agree to accept the invitation.

They began walking toward the hotel when the officer turned down a very narrow and dark street between buildings. "Oh, oh," Papa said, and he thought, "this is where I get it." He was carrying two suitcases, one which was tied with rope to keep it closed. Papa was frantically planning a manner of defense when the obvious assault happened. Halfway down the dark street, two young men jumped out of a dark doorway and jumped Papa, who began fighting for all he was worth. The officer shouted loudly and gruffly at the youths to leave Papa alone. The men turned and ran. Papa and the officer continued on toward the hotel. This rescue did not relieve Papa's wariness of the officer and what kind of trap he was being led into.

The officer took Papa up to a room on the fourth floor and, sensing Papa's fear, he said, "Don't worry, Joe, there are double locks on the door." When he left, Papa immediately went to the window to look for a possible escape, but there were no balconies or ledges to climb down and four floors was too high a drop to jump. Waking before five o'clock, Papa dressed quickly and quietly made his way down the stairs, sure that he would get out before anyone woke up. There in the lobby was the officer. He greeted my father and told him that he hoped to see Papa at the parade. Needless to say, Papa left the city as quickly as he could, and it wasn't until much later that he realized that the officer wasn't after him and might just have been kind to him.

The first thing that Papa did when he arrived in Cloz was to find someone who owned a car. Only one man did, the jeweler. Papa arranged to have this man drive him to the Switzerland border immediately if a war broke out. Papa ended up staying in Cloz for three months for a good long visit with his family, but did not unpack his suitcases for the first two weeks he was there. He was ever ready to make his way back to the United States, to his Paolina and his children.

Before leaving, however, he was out walking one day when he met his old teacher on the road and he told him, "You know, I never forgot that five in conduct you gave me." The teacher protested, "Now, Joe, that was a long time ago." Papa repeated, "I never forgot it." As a cousin from Cloz said years later, "Oh, I know that teacher well. He was a real austere man."

Finally it was time to return to America, and Papa took the opportunity on his way home to do a little sightseeing in Rome. He missed the bus he needed to go see the catacombs of the early Christians and martyrs. He amused himself while waiting for the next bus by watching a group of soldiers marching and changing guard in front of a building across the piazza. He had not seen any military marching since his time in the war and these soldiers were using a march step he had never seen before.

A well-dressed man came up to him and demanded to know why he was watching the building across the way. Papa told him he found it interesting to watch the soldiers march. The man asked why Papa was there. He explained that he was waiting for the bus to go see the catacombs. By this time, Papa could see that the man must be some kind of security or secret police. Next, the man asked Papa what he did for a living and Papa told him he was a laborer who worked in the cemetery. The man demanded, "Show me your hands."

After three months of resting and vacationing, Papa's hands were no longer hard, cracked and rough looking. The man told him that he didn't have a laborer's hands, and then he directed Papa, "Step into this area so I can check your papers." He was pointing to a narrow passageway between buildings. Papa countered, "If you want to check my papers you can do that right out here in the piazza." He handed over his wallet containing his passport. Inspecting the entire wallet, the man found the folded letter from the Italian Consulate. Unfolding it, he read the recommendation written about my father.

Handing everything back, the man immediately apologized. The Italian Consul must have been well known and highly regarded in Rome, and the letter must have spoken very well of my father. The man then offered to take Papa to personally meet Mussolini, but he declined, saying, "I don't have time. I want to go see the catacombs of the saints before I have to leave."

Papa returned to the United States and never returned to the old country again. His father died several years later, in 1941, at age seventy-three, and his mother died in 1947, at age seventy-nine. Papa said that now that his parents were dead he had no more desire to return to Cloz. I don't know why he never returned to visit his brothers and sisters, but I do know they always kept in close touch by mail. Mama did the writing mostly, and at times photographs and gifts were exchanged. Papa's youngest brother Lino, a Franciscan priest, came for a three-month visit in 1960 and again in 1980.

I would like to mention that Mama was constantly writing to someone. I told her she had a loving ministry of writing. She wrote to the old country to send news and keep in touch with family both on her side and Papa's side. She wrote to anyone experiencing difficulty, sickness, deaths, or sadness in their lives. She wrote to wish people well on so many different happy occasions, often writing late into the night. I remember Papa knocking on the bedroom wall with his knuckles and calling out to her, "That's enough, Paolina, come to bed." She received a lot of love by mail in return. I used to count the cards she received on her birthday or other special times. Sixty or seventy cards was quite common, and they came from Europe and the U.S.

CHAPTER 9

EARLY YEARS OF FAMILY LIFE

World War II started on September 1, 1939. I was born in 1938 so I'm not aware personally of what it was like or about rationing, but I remember life just post-war and my siblings remember both before and after the war. We all remember having plenty of food but not a lot of desserts. On Sunday, we had plain Jell-O for dessert. And there were always a lot of family and friends visiting, which was a lot of fun. This was a credit to our parents and extended family.

For our parents, those years of having and raising children were good and happy, but also difficult. Both Mama and Papa had surgeries or hospital stays for other reasons. After George, the fifth child, was born, there was a suspicion of cancer and Mama had radium treatments. I was born a year-and-a-half later. That must have been difficult, though she never said so. Frank was born six years later – he was the last child.

When I was about five-years-old, Mama had a helper. A large family, husband and parents to care for, a small apartment, illnesses, and economic tough times all finally physically wore Mama out. Papa hired an African-American woman to help her until she regained her strength again. I only remember that the woman was a large lady and very kind.

Papa was in the hospital for three months with excruciating sciatica pain. He also had other stays for surgeries later in life. I remember his return home after that three months. It was Christmastime and Papa had to lie on the couch. Mama got him a red Santa Claus hat and made a beard of cotton for him so he could play Santa Claus. In the early years, we each got one present at Christmas. I remember one year I received pajamas; another year a doll, the only one I ever received. She had a cloth body and beautiful ceramic face and hands. I kept her until I got married. One year, when I was about eight-years-old, I received a very big book of all the fairy tales, which started my love of reading.

On December 13th, we celebrated Saint Lucy's day or, as we called it, Santa Lucia. We all put out our shoes in front of our bedroom door and one of the grown-ups made a plate of polenta for Saint Lucy's donkey. Then we went to bed in anticipation of wonderful treats the next morning. We woke to shoes filled with marvelous candies, cookies, and a big orange.

I remember one cookie especially. It was shaped like an angel with a most beautiful angel decal on it, the size of the large cookie. There were so many wonderful and anticipated traditions in our growing years – First Communions, Confirmations, graduations, birthdays, weddings, the boys' high school football games, Italian Trentino Club parties and dances, relatives and friends visiting, the Feast of Our Lady of Mount Carmel. The happy times – the family fun was a constant.

But as I described before, the flat we lived in had four rooms, a bathroom and a pantry, and there were seven children, perpetually active. My brothers were chasing each other one day. Rounding a corner too fast in a high-spirited chase, they ran right into Mama's round glass china cabinet, sending it crashing to the floor. The cabinet and all her wedding gifts, bowls, vases, and good dishes were shattered. Broken! Everything!

Another time, I decided to sew on Mama's pedal sewing machine which she used to mend and sew new clothes for us. I wasn't supposed to, of course, so when I heard Mama coming I

I am pictured in the front in this picture, with George and Lino; in the rear is my sister Miriam, friend, Sophie, and Dominic

tried to grab the needle to stop it. Instead, I got the needle right through my nail and out the other side of my finger. I was about seven years old. Mama used that machine constantly and could sew beautifully. In one picture, the three older children –

Miriam with Archie and Dominic in the sailor suits Mama sewed for them.

Archie, Dominic and Lino – wore matching sailor style outfits which she made. Watching her sew seemed so wonderful that I wanted to do it, too.

We were always up to something, but we were good kids. We were being trained well. Every evening after dinner and before clearing the table, we all knelt down to say the rosary and other family prayers together. A lot of prayers were needed!

After we were finished praying one evening, Lino said, "Hey, Papa, I counted all the extra prayers we said on my rosary beads and we said enough for another whole rosary." This was not a good observation for Lino to voice. Papa gave him one of those "behave yourself" looks. We also said a prayer before meals and included a short prayer for the poor without food.

How great it was for us when a beggar came to our back kitchen door. Mama fixed him a drink and a big plate of food which he ate sitting on the steps leading up to the third floor. We were all excited to finally meet this poor person we always prayed for.

I would also like to add that we said our meal prayer in English but the prayer for the poor in Italian. What an advantage it was for us children; we spoke both languages at home. We spoke them simultaneously, often using both languages in the same sentence.

Another big part of our upbringing was strict adherence to obedience and respectfulness. You didn't hear gossip or swearing in our home. Papa also was the more strict of our parents. He was never cruel to us, but in a very quiet way he was strict and tolerated nothing but good behavior at home and school. In his late seventies, he wrote a letter to each of us children before entering the hospital for serious surgery. He apologized for being too strict with us when we were young, saying, "I'm sorry, but I didn't know how to be any different."

We were amazed and touched by his letter. Our image of him was so different than his. Yes, he made tough demands on us, but unspoken compassion and respect toward kids was apparent. We were proud to be Joe Rauzi's kids. His life taught him something which he passed on by the manner in which he treated us. It's summed up by one of his earnest remarks, "Remember the dignity of man."

My older brothers felt the strictness of Papa more than we two girls or Frank did. One of the older boys told Papa that he didn't like the fact that Papa never played with them. I guess my brother didn't understand the cultural training Papa had. As a matter of fact, I don't remember anyone's father playing with their children when we were young. After a while, Papa relaxed into American ways. It wasn't until he was forty-five and Frank was born that he started to play with his children. How he enjoyed Frank! He would get down on the floor and roll around with him when Frank was old enough for big boy roughhouse play.

In our young years, Papa would look at our report cards,

always checking the conduct and religion grades first. His only reprimand for poor grades was, "You can do better." He understood, as most parents did in the thirties, forties, and fifties, that you couldn't coddle kids. He also was not demonstratively affectionate with us children, but I often hear from others that in those days their parents weren't either, especially their fathers. There wasn't any hugging and kissing going on. In his later years, he was a totally different man.

As I mentioned before, bad behavior wasn't tolerated, but back in the thirties and forties the boys in our neighborhood were rough and tumble. It was important for a young guy to be strong and tough – or a very fast runner. Well, my brothers were part of that scene. Getting into trouble at school or in the neighborhood, however, didn't go over well with Mama and Papa.

One story explains well how bad behavior was dealt with immediately. There was a boy, Felix, who used to taunt Lino. He would hide and call out to Lino, "Lino, say son-of-a-bitch." He always made sure he was a good running distance from Lino. One morning, my brother was on his way to serve Mass at Mount Carmel Church and Felix was hiding behind some bushes and called out, "Lino, say son-of-a-bitch." That did it! Lino had lost his patience. The streets of Melrose Park at that time were made of bricks. He found a loose one and threw it at Felix, hitting him with it. Felix went howling home and Lino continued on to church to serve Mass.

At some point during or just after Mass, Lino felt a large hand grab the back of his shirt collar. Papa! Papa marched him over to Felix's house and once there he asked, "Lino, did you throw a brick at Felix?" "But Papa, he was trying to make me say a bad word," Lino protested. Papa repeated the question and Lino again pleaded for understanding of the situation.

Finally Papa said, "I ask you for the last time, did you throw the brick at him?" Lino said, "Yes," and Papa gave him a good smack. Then he asked, "What did he try to make you say?" "Son-of-a-bitch," Lino reported. Felix's mother asked Felix, "Did you try to make him say that?" Felix was laying on the couch, moaning and he wailed, "Yes." His mom gave him a good smack. The situation was over.

Not very often, but at times when the boys had really gotten into mischief or disobedience, Papa would send the offending boy to bed without supper. When Miriam thought no one noticed, she would sneak food into them. Years later, Papa told her he knew she was doing that. Doesn't that say a lot about his compassion for children?

One of the house rules we children didn't like but got used to was that we had to eat a bowl of the old country barley vegetable soup, menestra, before we were allowed to eat the rest of Mama's wonderful meals. I guess that's why we all grew up so healthy! One time, Dominic really didn't want to eat the soup and he was sitting at the end of the table near the stove. When he thought Papa wasn't looking, he quietly dumped his soup back into the kettle. Without looking up from his attention to his meal, Papa said, "Now you can eat two bowls, Dominic."

Speaking of supper, when Miriam and I were old enough to do so, we had to help Mama in the kitchen as she was preparing supper while the boys stayed outside playing. When Mama had the meal ready, Papa would go to the back window and give his whistle. Only Miriam could ever whistle as loud as Papa. The rule was that when you heard the whistle you were to be in the house within two or three minutes. Therefore, you needed to stay within hearing and running distance when playing. If the boys came really late, they had to kneel on the kitchen floor for ten or fifteen minutes before they could eat. If the matter of behavior was serious enough, we could expect a smack on our bottoms. This was typical of parenting in those days.

The only time I was ever corrected in this manner by my

father was when I was six-years-old, and I know it was so that I would never try that dangerous stunt again. What I had done was climb up on the flat overhang portion of the garage roof as I had seen my brothers do. Papa happened to look out the back porch window, and I excitedly waved and yelled to him thinking I had done a wonderful, brave feat. "Hey, Papa, look at me!" I've never looked at the world from the top of a garage roof again.

Despite all these stories of mischievousness and being disciplined, home was a wonderful place for us. One of the constants in our life was that Mama was always home taking care of us kids, Papa, and her parents. She went to shop with Papa, to church, and on occasion to visit someone. Otherwise, she was always there, and when we came home from school or play, we were greeted with wonderful aromas of good food cooking. She was an amazing cook. Despite all her cooking and cleaning, I never saw my mother look messy, no matter how hard she was working. She always looked clean and her hair was always combed nicely. Such dignity.

Mama had her hands full with us children when Papa wasn't there. When he was around, there was no misbehaving. The boys were good, but typical boys. Miriam was a quiet girl who had a lot of fun with the older brothers but was more quiet and very compliant toward Mama. She was Mama's joy, her first daughter, born on Valentine's Day. Miriam was six years older than I and always had me tagging along after her. I, on the other hand, must have been a dickens because I was in trouble a lot with Mama throughout my growing up years. I, however, thought I was a really good girl. This is a biased opinion, of course.

Active children were just one part of family life. There were many joys and many frightening times which needed prayers, such as when Archie was hit by a car and thrown thirty feet on his way to his very first day of school at age six. Blessedly, he recovered completely from his injuries and was always an excellent student. Archie was highly intelligent.

Another incident happened while we were in Michigan. The day after school let out in June every year from 1939 on, Uncle Joe would load up our things in his car and take Mama, our grandparents, and all us kids, some still babies, to Michigan. We stayed until the day before school started in September. Papa stayed home and worked.

The cottage on the lake was great fun, but for Mama it meant only cold water from a hand pump at the kitchen sink or outside. Buckets of water were kept by the indoor bathroom toilet for flushing, and any hot water needed was heated on the stove. She scrubbed clothes in a large metal tub with a scrub board which was set on a plank between two birch trees. I hope I'm not making Michigan and the cottage sound terrible. It was a wonderful place which Mama and all of us loved.

During one of our summers there, Mama had a strange feeling something was wrong because as she walked past a picture on the wall of a favorite saint, Saint Mother Cabrini, she felt the eyes of the picture were staring at her intently. She felt silly, thinking she was imagining things. But as she passed the picture again, the feeling was more intense. She knew something was wrong and quickly ran over to the beach several cottages away where we kids were swimming. As she was approaching, she saw Miriam go under the water twice, obviously in trouble because she couldn't swim well. The other kids were all playing and screaming playfully so they didn't see or hear Miriam. By the time she got to the beach, yelling for Dominic to help his sister, Miriam had gone under for good. Dominic dove under the water and kept pushing her up and toward shallow water. About nine years later, the day before Miriam entered the convent to be a nun, she, Papa and Mama went to a shrine of Saint

Mother Cabrini in Chicago to say thank you.

Another inconvenience was that without a car or driver for most of the summer in Michigan, Mama and Nona couldn't go to Sunday Mass. Noni would walk the five miles with us children. The boys took along their slingshots, trying to get birds and squirrels along the way. In their senior years now, they still hunt every fall. Not all the slingshot and BB gun hunting the boys did in Michigan met with approval.

One day Lino was in the woods for a long while and Mama was becoming concerned. He finally came home, the triumphant, great hunter, holding a dead skunk high in the air, shouting for all to hear, "Look at what I caught! I can sell the fur!" After Mama threw all his clothes on the roof of the cottage for the sun to kill the smell, she gave him a bar of strong soap and sent him into the lake to scrub the odor off.

When we returned home from Michigan in 1945, Miriam started high school, but not ordinary high school. She entered Nazareth Academy in LaGrange, Illinois, and also boarded there with the nuns, which allowed her to take part in their prayer-life and rule of the order of the Sisters of Saint Joseph. She always wanted to be a nun and this was an introduction to that goal. It was a hard letting-go for Mama and Papa even though they were happy for her and proud of her. Miriam was able to spend the summers at home, however.

CHAPTER 10

SAINT EULALIA YEARS

In 1949, my mother's brother, Doctor Bonfiglio Zanoni, came to visit my parents. He lived in Maywood, which was four miles away, and he went to Saint Eulalia's Church. Uncle Bonnie told them that Saint Eulalia needed a janitor. The job included the use of the old convent as part of the pay. It was a marvelous, two-story, wooden home with eleven large rooms, plus three full bathrooms and an enclosed porch. Then there was also a basement with a playroom, laundry, contina, and workshop.

Papa was torn by this decision. He couldn't bear leaving Melrose Park and Our Lady of Mount Carmel Parish where he was then working as a janitor, but he and my mom were raising a large family in such a small apartment. Uncle Bonnie was urging him to accept the job while at the same time keeping in touch with the pastor, Monsignor Martin Muzik, hoping he

Papa paints the church ceiling.

would hold the job for Papa. Finally, for Mama and the family, Papa accepted the job and a whole new era started for him. He was a few months shy of fifty years old.

For a while, Papa continued to be fairly active at Mount Carmel, but gradually his involvement was mostly the Feast of Our Lady, the Knights of Columbus, and the Holy Name Society. Slowly, life at his new parish replaced Mount Carmel. He remained always faithful to the work for the Feast of Our Lady, however.

His job at Saint Eulalia was total maintenance of a large school which housed more than six hundred children, and a

Papa at work at St. Eulia's school

smaller building which housed the primary grades, the church, driving the school bus, repairs at the rectory and new convent, snow removal, and lawn care around the entire complex. At first, the retiring janitor helped part-time. Older boys helped from time to time or in the summer. But for the most part, he did it all himself, including opening the church and preparing the altar for Mass before six o'clock in the morning, opening the school at that time also, and making sure the heating system was fueled.

At the end of the day, often very late into the night because of meetings and functions, Papa was there to check over the buildings and lock up everything securely. Papa also did all the painting needed in the school and the stripping and revarnishing of the classroom desks. He didn't go by a job description, he just did anything and everything needed to keep the church and school clean, repaired, and in good working order.

On weekdays and Sundays, Papa was always on the altar serving Mass or close by to guide the young altar boys in what they had to do. When Papa died, he had two funeral Masses. "I never knew anyone who had two funeral Masses!" one priest said. "Joe needed one more Mass to make a million," quipped

Mama and Papa, attending a church function.

Father Sullivan.

Aside from his job, Papa also helped Mama with their huge new home. Mama had a lot more house to clean, but she was so happy. Papa also cooked Sunday dinner more frequently now and always washed and waxed the floors, did the painting and washed the windows.

We children helped also. I remember thinking that my brother Dominic was so wonderful because when he came home from college for a weekend once in a while, he would mop the floors right away without being asked. I also remember Lino, home from college for the summer and in his late teens, was helping with the painting. While doing so, he was smoking and, hearing Mama coming, he quickly submerged his cigarette in the paint – clever, quick thinking. Nona and Noni were quite elderly by then and Miriam was gone, so I was Mama's housecleaning and ironing helper.

All this housecleaning discussion reminds me of one funny incident. When George was working with a construction company during the summer one year, he would come home, walk through the kitchen, down the hall and up the stairs to his room where he then undressed to take a shower. Papa told him not to track all that construction mess on his shoes and jeans through the house, that he should take those clothes off in the basement by going through the basement entrance. The next day, at suppertime, there was a knock at the basement door which led into the kitchen. For some unknown reason, my mother always kept that door locked. Papa was right behind me when I opened the door and there stood George, grinning, with nothing on but his underwear briefs. Papa just shook his head, saying to George, "There's women here," and walked away.

This was typical of Papa. When he wanted to correct you or teach you something, he said very little, usually one sentence and then expected you to live up to your responsibility or goodness. Papa has always been George's role model.

Miriam remembers one Lent when we were all very young. All the older kids gave up candy, and trading or reading comic books for Lent to offer as a sacrifice for Jesus. They stashed the candy and comics they got during Lent on a high shelf in the built-in cabinet on the back porch of our Melrose Park flat. On Easter Sunday, when Papa got home from church, the house was very quiet and he went looking for the children, finding them sprawled on the floor in the bedroom, reading comic books and eating all the saved candy. Papa asked what they were doing. When they explained that they were eating the candy they had saved and reading the comics they also saved during Lent, he said quietly, "Then you only gave God half."

On another occasion, when I was eighteen, I decided that there really wasn't anything difficult about driving a car – turn the key, put it in gear, step on the gas, and steer. I opened the two wooden doors to the garage that swung to the sides like shutters. Next, I confidently started the car and backed it out of the garage, knocking the right door right off the garage. Papa never said a word to me. Noni and he simply went out and repaired and rehung the door. He knew that no reprimand could equal my own miserable feelings. I stayed clear of car ignitions and gas pedals until I finally had to learn how to drive when I was thirty.

Now, returning to life in our new, big home, Mama used to be so delighted when the boys were home from college for the summers because they would often be upstairs in the huge dormitory-style bedroom at the front of the house, and naturally had their windows open. Often during these times, they would be singing together, all having good voices. Mama loved it and was so proud whenever she noticed the neighbors outside listening, or when they commented on the beautiful singing.

She was also delighted that a piano was left in the house

when we moved in. I started taking piano lessons at Saint Eulalia School. Whenever I played, right notes or terribly wrong notes, Mama was happy. She always wanted her children to play music. Whenever I played the piano for her through the years, she was so pleased and, believe me, I don't play very well, but her mother's heart heard differently! Then Frank started playing the drums when he was in his very young teens. In his adult years, he played drums professionally for a while. My folks not only bought him drums, they also put up with an amazing amount of loud playing for many years.

Before I go on with stories of us children and our beginning years in Maywood, I would like to tell of something that took place when Papa was in his mid-fifties. His parents had both passed away when later in the late 1950s Papa's family sent him the two portrait photographs of his parents that had hung in their bedroom. When they arrived, he was at work. My mother hung them in their bedroom. As soon as he came home she showed them to him. I followed to watch, expecting his delighted surprise. He didn't enter the room completely; instead, he stood

Lino, Papa in his 4th Degree K of C uniform, Sr. Miriam and myself.

just inside the doorway, resting his elbow on the high dresser next to the door and leaning his lips into the side of his left hand. He stood silent for a very long time as quiet, heavy tears paid homage to his love for his parents. I stood in the hallway watching him. My heart captured the scene forever. Mama stood there looking at him with a very compassionate look and was silent with him.

Fortunately for Papa and Mama also, there was a lot of family and family life to fill up the void he felt in the loss of his parents. But before too many years, we children began leaving to start our own adult lives. As each of us reached young adulthood, our parents no longer told us what to do. They just expected us to live as honest, good, and God loving people. They didn't tell us what we were to study in high school or college but trusted us and let us choose our own paths. Papa and Mama never told me I couldn't go, but they let me know they didn't think an acting career was for "nice" girls and they didn't like the idea of me applying to the Goodman Theater in Chicago, thinking it was so dangerous for a young girl to travel daily into the city alone. I didn't go. Other than that, we were all free to choose our own interests.

Miriam joined the convent the same year she graduated from high school in 1949. Mama and Papa missed her so much but were grateful to God and pleased when she entered and where she has happily been for fifty-four years, many of those years as a first and second grade teacher. I was married in 1959. Later, at the age of thirty-nine, when my own six children were in school, I returned to school and became a Licensed Practical Nurse. I also continue to enjoy performing in community theater.

All five of the boys met girls from Minnesota and moved there when married. Archie worked for an international company; Dominic became a teacher but left teaching to work with a mining company; Lino, who had a great deal of difficulty throughout his learning years because of dyslexia, became a teacher and the director for the remedial reading program for two school districts and authored books for that curriculum; George became a teacher; and Frank became a chef, often calling Mama for forgotten recipes or for advice.

The blessed thing about our varied lives is that we all are happy with our lives and careers. We are active in our communities and involved in church work and volunteering. We followed in Papa's footsteps, I guess. Sadly though, Archie died of

Papa and his five sons, left to right, Archie, Dominic, Lino, George and Frank.

an aortic aneurysm in 1998, and Frank died of cancer in 2003.

Besides us children, Papa adopted a whole new family and they in turn lovingly referred to him as "Mr. Saint Eulalia." To try to recapture his days at Saint Eulalia would take another whole book, so I'll just tell you the things Papa had to say and some insights of those years.

Monsignor Muzik, who hired Papa, was a loved, fatherly pastor who very definitely was in charge of all operations of the parish, as was expected of pastors in those days. Papa, respectful of priests, as always, did whatever Monsignor Muzik asked, but as time went on Papa's competence enabled him to claim his own work authority. His practical knowledge of buildings and work ethics were respected.

When Monsignor Muzik got the long-awaited new church built in the early 1960s, Papa really loved watching the construction process and the machinery used. He politely offered two suggestions where he saw potential problems in the future, but the architects and builders were confident in their plans. There were indeed problems in those two areas in later years. I don't know where he acquired that kind of knowledge of structure but he evidently had it. Our big convent house was torn down to make room for the parking area when the new church was built. Noni died in 1957 at age seventy-nine, so now there was only Nona. She, Papa and Mama moved into a small bungalow right next to the school and directly across from the side entrance to the church.

Besides loving his work, Papa loved the children and watched out for them. He didn't believe in dropping kids off the school bus on corners. He drove the bus route so that he could pull up right in front of their homes. When he was quite old, an older woman came up to him in church and asked, "Mr. Rauzi, do you remember me?" He apologized, "But you're a grandma. I'm sorry I can't." She told him her maiden name, hoping he'd remember. Papa said she was delighted because he knew immediately who she was and said, "Of course, you lived on 16th Avenue, the third house from the corner, a green house." He never forgot the kids. The woman hugged him so happily. He remembered her!

The children used to get pretty rambunctious on that bus after school, so Papa would start them praying. He would have them praying for all kinds of reasons and blessings. He led the prayers until there were only a couple of children left on the bus.

They took it seriously to pray for all the important needs with "Mr. Rauzi" and he was able to keep them safer because they sat quietly when praying. One day, however, the principal (with whom Papa had experienced some difficulty) came out to the bus and told Papa, "Mr. Rauzi, we don't believe in forcing children to pray." Papa responded, "Sister, in the school is your business. In the bus is my business," and the children and Papa contentedly kept on praying.

There was also fun on the bus. After Papa's funeral, a former student, Ed Ahern, wrote the following words in a letter to

> "It's hard to have anything short of fond memories of the man I knew simply as "Mr. Rauzi" throughout eight years of grade school. And I won't soon forget the times he repeatedly tried, in vain, to purposely hit at regular speed,

a notorious bump along Bataan Drive so that a bunch of us could play a vertical crack-the-whip in the last few rows. All year long he would be exceedingly careful to avoid that bump, slowly creeping over or around it. It was only during the final few days of the school year that he was going to let us have our fun. Much to his (and particularly our) chagrin, the city had finally decided to repair that stretch of road that week, putting a sudden and unceremonious end to his gesture. But that sense of charity – and humor – was not quickly forgotten."

Father James Quinlan on several parish matters:

At Christmastime, Papa had to keep a bushel in front of the bus which was filled twice over as each child got on the bus with brightly wrapped packages of cigars for Papa. The smoking he learned as a teenager during the war had gone from cigarettes to his ever-present cigar – and the children happily gave them as their gift to him.

Papa's love for these children was manifested in healing

Papa with the kids at a school function

compassion at times, as seen in these following incidents, and there are probably many more of which we are unaware. For many years, the children of the school attended Sunday Mass at nine o'clock in the morning at what was called the Children's Mass. All the children left their coats on long tables in the church hall downstairs and then filed in and out of church together. Someone started stealing from those coats. The faculty was trying to figure out how this was happening and by whom. Papa told them, "Leave it to me. I'll find out and end this stealing."

The following Sunday he stood in a corner niche by the confessional and just watched all during the Children's Mass. Before too long, a boy, about ten-years-old, got up and seemed to be headed to the bathroom. Papa let him go and then quietly made his way down to the church hall. There was the boy rifling through the coat pockets. Papa just stood there, waiting.

Finally, the boy saw him and froze. Papa told him where stealing would lead him in life. He then said to the boy, "I won't say anything to anyone, but you have to promise me that you will never steal again." The stealing ended. Many years later, a handsome young man approached Papa in church and identified himself as the boy who had been stealing. He then told Papa, "I came back to thank you. Today I have a college degree, a good job, a beautiful wife and three children. If it had not been for you, I would be in jail instead. By the time you stopped me from stealing, I was on my way to making a habit of it."

Papa also watched out for those boys who became troublesome in school or who he knew had difficult family trouble in their lives, such as the boy whose father ran off with his secretary. He was a prominent man in town and this left his wife to bear the shame and raise the children alone. Papa soon asked the boy to help with mopping the floors after school. He made him his helper so that he could show him respect and build up his self-esteem. Today that boy is happily married and a father, and owns several cleaning businesses. He brags, "Mr. Rauzi taught me the trade. He'd grab me by the back of the neck and say, 'No, no – this is the way you mop.'" Papa sent him a gag gift of a rag mop for his wedding.

Another boy he took under his protective wing became a police officer in the special forces. Papa was later godfather to one of his sons. As a married man, he and his wife and children treated Mama and Papa as their own family, and when Papa died I never saw a man cry as hard as he.

Papa also began a practice that continued for all his years at Saint Eulalia. On any day he chose during the last weeks of school, Papa would dress more formally and go visit the eighth grade class. The teachers let him have this time, no matter what was going on in the class at the time. He would talk to the kids, telling them that they were now grown up and much was expected of them. He then advised them on how to conduct their lives morally, responsibly, and always close to God. Having gone through so much during his own young years, Papa had a great concern for and need to encourage young people, especially young men whose self-esteem had been knocked down.

In his late years, the school children voted on and were honoring "living saints" on the Feast of All Saints. The fourth grade read the following of Papa, their chosen living saint:

> "He has taken loving care of God's house
> for a long time. He spends much time in
> the church, helping at many Masses and
> services, as well as praying and cleaning.
> Mr. Rauzi's house and heart seem always
> open to others. Children seem to be his
> specialty. We, the children, find him
> friendly, gentle, so nice, and never with a

> sad face. He always brings smiles to our faces. We believe that with all the love and affection Mr. Rauzi shows for God and His Church, for his own family and for all of us, God's children, he is a very good example of what Jesus wants of all of us on earth. Thank you, Mr. Rauzi."

Sister Mary Therese, who was in charge of Saint Eulalia School alumni activities, told me one day that she would send questionnaires to alumni coming back for a class reunion. One of the questions she would ask was "What is your most memorable memory of Saint Eulalia?" She said that up to seventy-five percent of the time the answer would be "Mr. Rauzi."

CHAPTER 11

THE LAST TWENTY-FIVE YEARS

About sixteen years into his job as janitor of Saint Eulalia, Papa's boss and friend, Monsignor Muzik, died. Six months later Monsignor William Quinn became pastor. He was a man dedicated to helping the poor, and had been active in helping the migrant workers obtain better wages and living conditions. Caesar Chavez was a close friend of his. His approach and friends, naturally, were more politically active. Saint Eulalia Parish had a hard time adjusting. Papa kept quiet and gave Monsignor Quinn all the respect he had always given to all priests. Slowly, Monsignor Quinn went through changes in his life and bonded with the people of the parish and the neighborhood, especially the poor.

Monsignor liked living simply. For this reason and because of an ever-growing friendship, Monsignor started coming over to Mama and Papa's house for lunch almost every day without any prearrangement. He knew it would be something simple and would usually include their old country barley vegetable soup. In their later years, Papa would most often cook the soup. He loved putting so many vegetables in it that the stirring wooden spoon would stand straight up in the pot.

Monsignor and Papa had lively discussions about stories of their lives, politics, or religion during these lunches – as well as good conversation and laughs. Papa was a very conservative person and Monsignor was more liberal. They would disagree strongly while trying to keep a respectful tone of voice. Boy, did they disagree! You could see the silent sparks fly! Their voices were restrained, but they maintained that respectfulness for each other. Eventually, Monsignor would even go up to Michigan to stay for a while with my folks at their little home up there.

Monsignor Quinn felt, when he first arrived at Saint Eulalia, that as pastor it was his duty to direct what was happening in the buildings. Once again, Papa had to go through another adjustment time until Monsignor understood that the buildings and workings of the parish property were in good hands with Joe Rauzi.

I enjoy this story Monsignor Quinn told me one day. He was at a large important gathering in Chicago when a man came up to him and said enthusiastically, "You're the pastor of Saint Eulalia." Monsignor said he was feeling rather pleased at being recognized in this enthusiastic manner when the man continued, "I know your janitor, Mr. Rauzi."

On August 15, 1978, Monsignor was a part of the wonderful occasion of Mama and Papa's fiftieth anniversary. The celebration started at a Mass at Saint Eulalia and continued at a restaurant. Mama and Papa were surrounded by their children and grandchildren, except our brother Lino (who was in the hospital in Minnesota) and his family. A surprise phone call from Lino was arranged during the dinner, so that all of Mama and Papa's children would be present to them. Also gathered were about two hundred and fifty relatives and friends.

In preparation for the fiftieth, Mama and I went shopping for her outfit for their great occasion, and she said to me, "I wanted a long dress when Papa and I got married." So now we set out to find one for this joyful anniversary. We did find one and it must have been meant for her to have. It was simple, full-length, elegant, and cream-colored like her wedding dress. Perfect!

I would like to add one last (but unrelated) story Papa told me about his early years at Saint Eulalia. When Papa was in his very late fifties his enduring physical strength saved his life. He was painting the walls extending up the stairwell in the school which led up to the second floor. He was on an extension ladder near the second floor banister when he lost his balance and, while falling, grabbed the banister, flipping himself completely over. Now he was hanging over the stairwell clutching the banister backward. He managed to pull himself up to safety. He maintained his strength and capacity for long hours of hard work well into his seventies.

I have been recounting many stories of Papa's relationship with the school children and pastors, but not about the rest of the priests and nuns or the adult parishioners. Many times Papa would not agree with the ideas or decisions of various committees. When he felt he was right he held his ground or backed away in silence from the necessary politics of people. If asked his opinion, however, he gave it without holding back. He also had an easygoing friendship with so many parishioners. You could readily see they liked and respected one another, often joking with each other. Papa was happy in his friendships. He enjoyed them! I saw how they watched out for each other and helped each other and prayed for each other.

Papa and Mama's home became a gathering place over the years. The parish priests were often guests for dinner when my parents had special guests, such as visiting Italian missionaries. Once, my uncle, Father Silvio Zanoni, Mama's brother, brought home one of the Auxiliary Bishops of Chicago for a home-cooked Italian meal. Then there were also some of the Sisters who taught school at Saint Eulalia who became very dear friends.

On one occasion, the parish priests were not included for one of Mama's special dinners. I was always in the kitchen because I served the dinners for Mama. One of the assistant priests, Father Raynor Richter, very quietly knocked at the kitchen door, knowing I'd be there. He whispered, "I saw all the cars, I knew your mom was cooking a big dinner." I quietly served him dinner in the kitchen. He left at dessert time so he wouldn't be discovered. We laughed about that many times. Father Richter's "at home" ease with coming into our kitchen was not an unusual thing, as seen every weekend.

After the Sunday Masses, friends, priests, deacons and their wives who had been at Mass would stop in to visit before going home. Often whole families stopped in. The coffeepot was constantly brewing yet another pot of coffee, and there was always an amazing amount of coffee cakes and cookies served. Every Sunday this was the norm. Mama kept tins of cookies, pastries, and cakes on the stairs leading up to the attic for these gatherings.

My sister and aunt would arrive home from the convent for their Sunday visit and would hope they could get through dinner, which was usually at one o'clock, before more company started arriving. Very often they were not able to accomplish that. Old country friends, uncles, aunts, cousins, and good friends visited all day long.

No formal arrangements were ever made for these visits. There would be new people arriving all day and into the evening. This was every Sunday. People just came, knowing there would be welcome, good visiting, and good desserts. They often came bringing those desserts. Conversations were wonderful to hear and be a part of. Old life memories and stories were told, jokes – a lot of jokes – political issues, troubles in life, opinions on just about anything, news and, of course, Papa's stories. What a rich tradition those Sunday gatherings were!

When Papa died and Mama moved out to the convent with my sister, some of the relatives and friends questioned with loss in their voices, "Where are we going to gather now?" Interestingly, they all used the same phrase. We never did gather like that again.

When my parents spent the summers in Michigan, their little house there was also "the gathering place." Daily, and sometimes twice daily card games, whole tables of friends and relatives sitting around having coffee and desserts, sometimes dinner, and even visits from some of the nuns, priests, deacon, and friends from Illinois.

What a gift of welcome, hospitality and fun my parents gave to others. Also, compassion and comfort, as many came seeking just that. There was also another aspect to these gatherings of family and friends, and that was the "family historian – Mama." She forever was clicking away with her camera or turning on her tape recorder, wanting to capture these wonderful moments. As a result, we now have voices captured on tape of loved ones deceased long ago and pictures of so many happy times and dear people.

Before I go on with Saint Eulalia days, I want to relate a wonderful Michigan story Papa told me. Remember I told you about Papa's friend, Rica, who he used to yodel to from the mountain slopes and she would respond? Well, when Papa was semi-retired and started to spend summers in Michigan with Mama and Nona, the first thing he did was take a walk along the road above the first of two hollows created by the previous mining years – and at the bottom was the lake. As he was walking along, he saw his friend of many years past, Rica. She had immigrated to Norway, Michigan. When Papa saw her, she was working in her garden. He yodeled their signal yodel to her and as she stood up, without yet turning around to look, yodeled back the correct response. He enjoyed that moment so very much and told the story with delight and fun written all over his face.

Returning to the stories of Papa's last twenty-five years and Saint Eulalia, time brought yet another pastor to Saint Eulalia who would be one of the regular visitors at Papa's and Mama's home. Father Jim Quinlan came as an assistant to Monsignor Quinn, eventually becoming pastor himself when Monsignor retired and became pastor emeritus. He was in his young thirties when he left a successful business career to enter the priesthood.

He and Papa were good friends. They respected and admired each other. Papa observed and liked the way Father Quinlan lived his priesthood and physically worked so hard in

Papa "steals the act" at the parish dinner dance.

and for the parish. He, like my father, also loved planting flowers and trees, and he did much to beautify the grounds. Father Quinlan also beautifully redecorated the church and repaired and renovated the school buildings. But most of all, Papa admired his devotion to his priesthood and his amazing sermons.

We have a picture of Father Quinlan laughing in enjoyment of Papa. It was at the annual parish dinner dance which Father initiated in the parish. He also started the tradition of honoring a man or woman of the year at these banquet events. Much to Papa's surprise, he was chosen for the honor the first year it was held. He stood up and walked to the bandstand to receive his plaque amid the applause. Father Quinlan intended to simply hand the award to him and say a few words about Papa but, instead, Papa politely reached for the microphone and quite comfortably took over, giving one of his "talks." Father Quinlan just stood there in delight and laughed – thus our photograph.

Msgr. Muzik

Msgr. Quinn

Fr. Quinlan

The transition phase of yet another new priest and pastor to adjust to went more smoothly with Father Quinlan, as he wrote in the Sunday church bulletin after Papa's death, which you will read at the end of this book.

Papa was already in his "somewhat" retirement years when this new young priest arrived. I say somewhat because at age seventy, Papa had to retire, which was mandatory for employees of the Chicago Catholic Diocese. He was still working from six o'clock in the morning till late at night and had no intentions of quitting, but it was mandatory. Papa had always been so conscientious about taking care of the buildings, the machinery, and the bus. It wasn't a job, it was a personal commitment. He told me with a grin that I couldn't quite tell was mischievous or just happy, "I only got one complaint about the buildings that I can remember. One lady said I waxed the floors too much and she had a hard time walking in her high heels because they were slipping."

Now he was told that he had to walk away from this important part of his life. He asked the pastor, Monsignor Quinn at the time, to please allow him to continue just to take care of the church. He insisted that they didn't have to pay him, just let him take care of God's house. The pastor agreed, but he decided to give Papa a small thank you check each month. He also told Papa and Mama that they could continue living in the house the parish gave them to use for as long as they wanted.

With less work to do, Papa could often be found sitting in church visiting with Jesus. Ten years after his death, Mama's dementia allowed her to forget that "her Joe" died and she kept asking for him. I would always tell her he went to the store. She was fine with that response, but one day I said that he was in church praying. "He's always in church," she said, somewhat annoyed. Those visits with Jesus lasted up to an hour and might happen at least twice a day.

CHAPTER 12

TRANSITION TO HEAVEN

In May of 1987, my parents sat in our kitchen in Green Bay, Wisconsin. During our yearly trip to pick them up in Illinois to take them to their house in Michigan, they stopped for a couple of days to visit. Papa decided to give me all his wishes for his funeral, which I was to write down. Mama was appalled. She didn't like talking about death, and Papa and I were not only discussing it, we were also laughing and talking quite easily about it. She thought we were terrible.

A real confrontation happened during our conversation. Papa said, "Tell the people – no flowers. Tell them to give the money to the poor." Mama was perturbed. "Now, Joe!" Papa interrupted her, "Paolina, this is what I want." She countered, "When people are married, the two become one. I have a right in this decision, too." I tried to arbitrate, suggesting, "Papa, people need to grieve the way they have to. Maybe giving flowers is something they need to do." Mama cheered, "You tell him, Sylvia!" Papa's voice now was firm. "No." The matter was dropped.

On August 15, 1988, all seven of us children and everyone in our families gathered in Norway to celebrate Papa and Mama's sixtieth wedding anniversary. Father Jim Quinlan drove the five-hour trip up to Michigan to celebrate their anniversary Mass and be with us for a weekend of festivity. They would celebrate three more years of this lasting love. The summer of their sixtieth was the last healthy and carefree sum-

THE GOOD WORD

Dear Friends,

Last week I packed off my dog (to one of my sisters), packed a small bag for myself and drove 6 hours to the Upper Peninsula to a little town called Norway. This small, old world Michigan town has been the summer home (for over 40 years) for two people of our parish who have come to mean much to me and to many other Eulalia parishioners. I embarked on such a journey to celebrate the awesome achievement of 60 years of sacramental wedded life for Joe and Paulina Rauzi. These two permanent fixtures of our parish were married on the Feast of the Assumption, August 15, 1928 -- how appropriate, since they both have a deep and abiding love for the Mother of God. Together, they have given life and love to 7 children, 6 of whom are married with so many children that I forgot the number (and some of their children have children themselves). Joe and Paulina are also blessed to have a daughter in religious life. It was so evident to me during my three-day visit, just how blesssed their family is. They have been nurtured and sustained at the table of the Lord and they have, in their parents, living witnesses of God's only Son's Gospel of love

We celebrated in so many wonderful ways during my stay but the apex of Joe and Paulina's anniversary came when we gathered around the table of the Lord and shared the banquet of God's love for us in the sacrifice of the Mass.

Joe wouldn't let me renew the vows spoken 60 years before; he said he spoke them once and for ever, so there was no need to do it again. What they both wanted was a special blessing which came, first, from Cardinal Bernardin (who sent a letter of congratulations and two rosaries blessed by The Holy Father) and, secondly, from myself since I was priviledged to offer Mass for them along with their summer pastor at St. Barbara's Church in Norway. As you can see by these three pictures of before, during and after the Mass, the life, love, spirit, faith and devotion of Joe and Paulina is a wonder and a beauty to behold.

Again, God's choicest blessings in this life and eternal reward in the next.

Fr. J.

mer Papa would spend in Michigan.

I would like to add a couple of examples here of their feelings for each other. At one point, Mama was in the hospital in the late winter and Papa wanted to bring her a bouquet of her favorite flowers, forget-me-nots and daisies, which were definitely out of season. They would have to be flown in and would be quite expensive. Papa said, "I don't care the cost, I want Mama's favorite flowers for her." They were in their senior years at the time.

The summer Papa died in Michigan we had just come home from morning Mass when I mentioned to Mama that I noticed that some of the ladies at church really fuss over Papa. (He was still handsome in his old age, and nice.) She put one hand on her hip and wagged her finger with her other hand, saying, "Yes, and I know who it is, too!" Boy, was she irritated! She was eighty-three and he was ninety-two.

In October, 1989, Papa's journey toward heaven started. At age eighty-nine, he had a heart attack. Over the next three years his health declined. These were difficult years for Papa for several reasons. He hadn't driven a car for several years but was still getting around to do errands and grocery shop. Now, he was confined pretty much to their home and church. He missed being out and about. Our cousin, Herman, would deliver their groceries from his store, and many kindnesses, too. Also, watching other people do the work he used to do made him sad. "I wish I could do that," he'd say. At other times he'd say, "These four walls are my prison."

So Sister Miriam and I had a goal of making him laugh when he would get too down. Being depressed often is the case when a person is gravely ill. His little blue parakeet, Lucky, was good for Papa because he enjoyed feeding and playing with

Mama and Papa in Michigan two weeks before he died.

him, cleaning his cage, and teaching him to talk. Lucky could say, "Good morning, Paolina. Give me a kiss. Our Father who art in heaven." It occupied Papa, who loved him. Mama gave the bird away to a young godchild as soon as Papa died because Lucky sounded just like Papa and she couldn't bear it.

Mama and Papa over the years.

Papa loved babies and all children. He enjoyed them so much ! Here, Papa shares a smile with our first child, Monica.

Papa enjoys a good time with our youngest child, Kathleen.

Thank heavens the Sunday visitors still came. They were a lifeline to him. Also, Sister Miriam called every night to visit and say goodnight to him and Mama. This was a special part of their evening and she was their joy. Phone calls from the rest of us children gave them the love they needed so badly now. When I called every Sunday, I had a new joke prepared for them, which they loved. Having all five sons living in Minnesota was a hard part of life for my parents.

Since I used to live right down the block from them it was even worse when we moved off to Wisconsin, taking our six children they enjoyed so much so far away. While I'm grateful for all of my life, looking back I know that if I had more wisdom at the time I would not have moved away from them in their senior years.

More than once, I heard Papa say, "I wish I had at least one of my sons close by to help me." Nona also died in 1975, so in their late years it was just the two of them.

Dear and good family and friends stepped in for us children. Now in these senior and, later, more difficult years, Uncle Bonnie and Uncle Joe, Mama's brothers; and dear friends Lydia and Guilio Camerini watched over our parents even more than they already had. They helped them with financial papers and whatever else they needed. Fortunately, I was able to drive home frequently and would take them to most of their doctor visits or hospital stays. The boys visited whenever they could. Miriam came, sometimes more than just Sundays now that she was no longer teaching.

My parents didn't go to Michigan the summer after Papa's heart attack; he was too weak. Papa's days passed quietly and he was happy for Monsignor Quinn's lunch visits. A lot of praying also occupied his time. He had the habit of sitting at the end of the livingroom couch near the archway leading into the dining room, reading all his prayers from his old, worn out prayer book. Its pages had been glued and taped so much that they were thick and stiff.

Pages were also smudged and worn to ragged edges from the years as he thumbed his way through prayers of love and petition for everyone. Actually, this was his second prayer book. He completely wore out the first one. His sight was so bad that he couldn't read the prayers but recognized which ones they were by the pages and he'd say them by memory. I have that prayer book now and I keep it on my bedside table where I look at it and remember his love and faith.

Speaking of Papa's faith life, I observed something in his last years. He loved sweets and I noticed for quite a few years that he never ate any sweets during the week, only on Sundays. I knew he was offering this fasting sacrifice and discipline in prayer, or as an act of love to God. Then in his last year, he refused sweets even on Sunday, and I argued with him. "Papa, it's Sunday, God's day. You should at least have a dessert on Sunday." He responded with almost sorrow in his voice, "No, I never did anything for God." And he never ate sweets again. What an amazing statement and humbleness from a man who lived entirely with the love for God as his life-motivating force.

For his dessert, he would cut up an apple with a table knife or his pocket knife. Sometimes it was other fruits that were in season. He liked apples as they brought back memories of the apples his town of Cloz was famous for. As an adult, he would often bring me a Golden Delicious apple because he knew I liked them, and he would wrap them in foil like the famous golden apples in Cloz are wrapped.

We have a picture of Papa sitting on the porch in Michigan holding a small twig of an apple tree with five beautiful, perfect apples clustered on it. That cluster of apples pleased him so much that we took a picture of him with them.

The following year brought another exceptionally hard five

Papa, with a perfect cluster of five apples. It reminded him of the apples in Cloz.

weeks in the hospital, this time on a respirator for twenty-one days. We almost lost him one night but a wonderful young doctor, Doctor Michael Deprest, took great care, and we were able to bring Papa home, this time with a pacemaker embedded in his chest.

There were letters and comments from doctors and some staff about how Papa had touched their lives. One doctor, who had been very clinical whenever in the room discussing Papa's condition with his med students in tow, met Papa and I as we were leaving the hospital. My father must have penetrated his veneer because he threw his arms around Papa, telling him how happy he was to see him able to go home.

Papa's energy and life improved. One day he surprised us by announcing, "I never had my cataracts taken out because I was too old and I thought I would die soon anyway. But now after all that happened and God didn't take me yet, I guess I'm going to get them out." A doctor who specialized in eye surgery for high-risk patients was found and he was careful with Papa. It was a wonderful success. The day after the surgery we returned to the hospital where the doctor removed the bandage and asked Papa, "What can you see, Joe?" Mama was sitting at the opposite end of the room and Papa looked straight at her and said, "How cute."

However, when we got home again, Papa kept looking at me curiously. Finally he said, "You got old, kid." I protested, "How come Mama gets a 'cute' and I get an 'old'?" Besides not seeing my aging process, we were surprised at other things he hadn't seen in many years. There was a large oil painting of his church in Cloz, which we children gave my parents at their fiftieth anniversary, hanging on the livingroom wall. He stared at it, amazed. In the last twelve years, he never really saw it.

The following spring Papa again surprised us by announcing that they were going to Michigan. I protested because he was very obviously close to his last days. He insisted. "I want to give Mama one more year in Michigan." He wanted to give "his Paolina" this last gift of joy. I can still see them in my mind's eye – Papa always reaching for Mama's hand as they walked along or when posing for a picture.

With a call to our friends who lived across the road from them in Michigan, Walter and Lois Belmore, the plans were set. Walter and Lois took the shutters off, opened the house, got the utilities and water and phone turned on, and cut the grass, just like they did every year for Papa and Mama, simply because they are good people and good friends. I reluctantly went to Illinois to pick them up, knowing that Papa should not leave home and his doctors. He just said to me, "Die here, die in Michigan, die in the car, what's the difference?" I teased him back, "Papa, it matters to me because I'm driving!" Making him laugh was an important mission.

A letter I wrote to my sister and brothers after I got them settled in Michigan says volumes. I found a copy of it among my papers a couple of months ago. I think I'll let the letter introduce the end of Papa's life to you. But let me say first that at some time in that last year before going to Michigan, Papa gave his black silk wedding suit away to the poor. He had kept it and his white silk bow tie he wore on their wedding day for sixty-three years. He was now beginning to relinquish things that were important to him on this earth and was preparing for heaven.

NORTHWOOD HO !

Dear Sister and Brothers,

I have been soaking in some priceless moments and conversation with Papa and Mama these last days. I think you all should have the benefit of knowing these moments.

I arrived in Maywood early Tuesday, 22nd, and the Saint Eulalia parking lot was filled with carnival equipment. Each day brought more booths till the carnival started Thursday evening. Papa loved it! He and I went out to walk through the grounds countless times and he kept coming up with stories of his days of through the years of the "Festa de La Madonna."

Then he'd say he wished he could be working to help the Saint Eulalia carnival instead of watching. He was frequently at the back window and asking me if it was going good – if people were coming. Finally, Saturday night he got Mama out there. Holding hands, he walked her through the entire carnival. They laughed and visited with friends, enjoying themselves so much!

On Friday, on the way to pick up Miriam, we drove through Queen of Heaven Cemetery and said prayers at Nona, Noni, and Father Silvio's graves. On Wednesday, I took Mama and Papa to pray at the Greek church with the crying Madonna icon. Both times Papa thanked me so much for providing an opportunity to do these things. Both were so important to him. That evening, Julio Camerini made sure to talk with me privately to tell me that Doctor Kroeger was apprehensive about Papa leaving the area. After a couple of months of trying to persuade them not to go, this information made me feel helpless.

On Saturday morning, Papa and I went to Mass at the chapel of Our Lady of Mount Carmel and said the rosary. After Mass, Papa went to confession in Italian. Being so faithful to Saint Eulalia and Father Quinlan, he offered me an unnecessary explanation that it's good for him to go to confession in Italian sometimes so he can express himself better. This was an important confession for him and he wanted to get all his thoughts out.

As we headed for home, he said, "Let's go past the old house on 24th to see how the new people fixed it up." He leaned toward the window, intently looking at our old house. Then he said with a sneaky grin, "The grape vines are still alive. You know, I stole those vines back in the thirties from the yard of an old condemned house." We then drove very slowly down the block and Papa commented all the way, pointing out where he and Mama lived across from Gerolome when they were first married. He talked about different friends as we passed their homes. At the end of the block, almost in tears, he thanked me. I believe, in his mind, this was a last pilgrimage.

Saturday evening, as Mama, Sister Miriam and I were sitting at the table with him, Papa thanked us for taking care of him over this difficult couple of years. Then he asked us to forgive him for the times he was irritable. Next, he again gave us funeral instructions. Having said all he was going to, he turned to Mama and said, "Come on, Paolina, we'll go out to the carnival." To which she replied, "Great, first you ask our pardon and then you talk about funerals and then you ask me to out to a carnival!" Can you just hear her!

Sunday morning, after the Masses, there was a constant stream of well wishers in the house, laughing, hugging, kissing. I packed the car and finally we were ready to go. Papa came out first and was alone for a while. I knew he didn't notice me standing at the front door of the house. He stood beside the car, took off his hat and put it on the hood of the car along with his cane. He pulled up his shoulders and stood very erect, facing the sanctuary of the church. He stood very still, then genuflected the best he could, and got in the car. He was saying goodbye to his beloved Jesus in the church he loved so much. Mama and I came out shortly after and Miriam waved us off. As we rounded the block, Papa verbally admired all the planting Father Quinlan had done. Papa thinks the world of him.

Our very happy trip had begun! They napped a while for the first forty miles as I made my way through an awful lot of Chicago Memorial Day traffic – slowly. Then the farmland started and Papa's joy began to unfold. Because of his cataract surgery, he could see the scenery for the first time in years and he just loved the neat and orderly farm fields, barns and silos. When I pointed out something particularly interesting one time, he said, "Don't worry, Sylvia, I'm taking it all in." Covering one eye at a time with his hanky, he checked his vision, then he said, "For years I never saw all this beauty and scenery. I think God wanted me to make this trip just so I could see it! God is too good!"

Going through Milwaukee, I said something outrageous to Papa, who was drinking coffee at the time. He sputtered coffee everywhere as he broke out in laughter. Mama was a riot in the back seat because you know how she shakes all over when she laughs hard with that "Sneaky Dog" laugh. Dominic could really get them laughing, too, when he would call every week.

Well, anyway, Papa was in good spirits and kept up a running dialogue. Finally he said, "We're almost there, aren't we?" I answered, "Darn, Papa, I wanted to sneak you into Green Bay and surprise you that we were already home. How did you know?" Pointing to his watch, he said, "I figured it by my watch. You're making good time, kid." He also gave me a 4-Star rating on my driving. From Papa, that's something! You know what a careful driver he has always been.

My whole family was there to greet us when we arrived in Green Bay. We ate dinner, took pictures – naturally – and began the last leg of our journey to Michigan at five o'clock. The first stretch of pine trees started comments from Papa which culminated with "Paolina, we made it, now we're in Michigan." On the way in to Norway, we stopped (but didn't get out of the car) to say hello to their good friends, Maria DelMoro, the Cescolini's, Peripauli's and Belmores. Such happiness! This was the first year we didn't have to stop for Papa's leg cramps because I insisted he sit in the front seat for leg-stretching room, and it worked. Thank God.

On Monday, we went to Mass and then did their grocery shopping. After supper, we went to see Uncle Joe and Aunt Catherine and the new construction at the resort. While standing near the shore and looking out over the lake, Papa began to cry. He could see all the houses around the lake and even could see people entering their cottage across the lake at the point! His new sight is a never-ending joy and amazement to him.

I was going to do some flower planting, but there was no way I was going out near or under any trees! Papa laughed so hard at me as I shuddered at the sight of two army worms he whipped off my sweater. On Tuesday, I finally did plant flowers.

Papa did an army worm check on me every few minutes. This was a definite act of brave love, folks. That's not bragging but an explanation. I'm still a city girl. Green Bay has not put the country in me yet.

Papa is weak and walks with his cane all the time now to steady himself. I remember just a couple of years ago when a friend in his late thirties or early forties came to visit. He and Papa were doing the typical male teasing – "Let's see who's stronger" challenge by gripping each other's hands. Papa did - n't even exert an obvious straining as he held the man's hand. Within seconds, Papa's friend was down on one knee.

It's still cool in Michigan. One morning I woke up freezing. It was in the thirties and it didn't help that Mama was playing Christmas music on her boom box! I kid you not!

I would like to end by mentioning that perhaps you can see how very much Sister Miriam and I are blessed because we have the opportunity to have day to day wonderful (and sometimes difficult) times with Papa and Mama.

Love, Sylvia

Summers in Michigan were full of visits from family and friends, Sister Miriam, the boys and their families. I went back and forth every weekend or more, since I was only a couple of hours drive away.

Papa tended to his Finch bird feeder outside the kitchen window. He loved those birds and his pet, Lucky. He loved going to the feed mill to buy seeds for them. He also continued playing cards with neighbors and relatives, but was no longer sharp at it. For the first time ever, I started throwing the games to let him have the fun of a win. Papa also greatly enjoyed it when little children came to visit. For many long years, Papa always played a game with little children. They would hold up their little hands in folded praying fashion and Papa would roll their

Our family at David's wedding. In back row, left to right, are Frank, Lino, Sylvia, Dominic, Archie and George. Sr. Miriam Dolores sits with Mama and Papa in front

tiny hands between his big strong hands while he sang a little warbling sound. They loved it! It was not unusual to see a child run up to him with folded hands.

On August 17th, my brothers brought Papa and Mama down to Green Bay for our son David and Jill's wedding. I arrived in church well beforehand and saw them sitting in the front pews. I sat in the pew in front of them so I could turn to talk with them. When I caught the first glimpse of Papa's face, I inadvertently drew in my breath. Wedding preparations had kept me away from Michigan for a couple of weeks. I was shocked to see the change in him. Seeing the look on my face, he quickly put a finger to his lips, silently telling me not to say anything.

Later that day, as family and guests visited at our home while waiting for time to leave for the reception, Papa lay on David's bed, resting. He asked for all of us, his seven children, because he wanted to talk to us together. He told us to stay close to each other, to love and help each other. He then repeated his often given advice – not to work on Sunday for profit, only to help a poor person in great need.

As summer proceeded, Papa's health was very obviously declining and I kept suggesting that we return to Illinois, but Mama didn't see what my nursing-trained eyes could see, and Papa, for her joy, was determined to let her stay until fall as usual.

During the first week of October, I went into Illinois with my husband who was attending a retiree event at his old company, Commonwealth Edison. I decided I'd better get Mama and Papa's house cleaned real well, knowing the inevitable would soon be happening. It was past midnight when I finished cleaning.

When we arrived back in Wisconsin early the following day, I called my parents because I was supposed to go to Michigan that day to take Papa to the doctor the following morning. I asked my mother if I could just come up early the next morning because I was so tired. She answered, "You better come, Sylvia, Papa has been waiting for you for two days." I grabbed a few pieces of clothes and left immediately. I knew.

Papa was sitting in an easy chair in the livingroom when I arrived. We didn't say anything to each other. I just knelt down and lifted his pants leg and saw that his normally slender ankles and legs were grossly swollen, all the way up to his knees. He coughed and put a hanky to his mouth. Opening up the hanky, he showed me bright red blood. He said quietly, "It's been like that for two days." He wanted to let life happen; he didn't want to go to the doctor until his appointment the next morning. He slept sitting up in that same chair so he could breath. The next morning he said, with a tone of endurance and victory, "I made it one more night."

For the first time, Mama helped him get dressed. He was so weak. He had showered, shaved and dressed by himself all through the past three years – now he couldn't. He walked with two canes that morning. As we were leaving, he tossed me a spoon. I asked him what it was for. He said that he lost his shoehorn and his feet were too swollen to get into the shoes. I was to use it as a shoehorn at the doctor's office.

Mama came along because she wanted to go to the drugstore and the grocery store while we were at the doctor's office. She still could not or would not look at the finality of Papa's condition. Papa just looked at me, saying silently with his eyes, "Just let her do it." He didn't want to alarm her.

As soon as the doctor came into the room, I told him what was happening and asked him to please call Doctor Kroeger in Illinois. He checked Papa over briefly and left to call. I sat on a small stool next to Papa and we held hands – something we had never done before. We didn't speak. The doctor came back and said softly so that my father wouldn't hear since his hearing was poor, "Your father is dying." I responded, "I know and he knows." He then gave us the option of getting in the car without stopping to pack and try to get to Illinois before anything happened, or to put Papa in the hospital. After the last long and difficult stay in the hospital, Papa vowed he'd never enter one again, but now he said quietly that he would go to the hospital.

Mama arrived at the doctor's office from her shopping. When we told her Papa had to go into the hospital, she was very concerned that he have a bed by the window so he could look out. He indeed had a window bed and directly across the street was Saint Mary's Catholic Church – Jesus. Also the trees that fall were spectacular – so golden that they caused a lovely warm yellow glow in Papa's room.

I called my sister Miriam right away, who then called our brothers, relatives and friends. All the boys left Minnesota as quickly as they could, hoping to get to Michigan in time to say goodbye to Papa. Unfortunately, they didn't make it. I kept Sister Miriam updated every couple of hours, as she was so hurting and wanting to be there. She kept everyone informed.

Papa seemed relieved to be in the hospital. He sat there thanking God for all He had done for him and for the beauty of the fall trees. At times he would say, "If I ever offended anyone, I'm sorry." He kept looking over at Mama and smiling with such tremendous love that I felt I had no right to watch this personal and intense love he was emitting toward her. He was peaceful and seemed sweetly happy – totally unafraid.

I left for a few minutes to go to the cottage to get Papa's old, worn prayer book, then I took Mama to afternoon Mass, bringing Holy Communion to Papa when we returned. Papa read all his prayers in his prayer book as usual that day. He lived his last hours as he always had.

When they brought Papa his supper tray, it was fish, his favorite. He ate the whole meal and then told me in an urgent and knowing manner, "Take Mama home and make sure she eats real good." He knew what the next days would bring her and knew she'd need her strength. Mama was still not aware that these were his last hours or she would never have left his room. As we were leaving, Papa said, "Paolina, aren't you going to kiss me goodbye?" She kissed him and then Papa just looked over at me. Again, so much was said in that look – in those few seconds.

I cooked quickly and we got back to the hospital as soon as possible, finding Papa up in a recliner chair with an IV. He was tiring. A nurse came in, followed by the doctor around seven o'clock in the evening. She administered a shot to try to get some of the water out of his system. As soon as the shot was injected, his body reacted fiercely and he knew he was leaving Mama. Looking at her with shocked awareness, he called out to her, "Paolina, I'm going, I'm going, I'm going." His wonderful face went into spasm and he lay unconscious. This was actually a blessing for Mama because for the next five hours she was able to cry, to realize his death, to pray over him and bless him. It was a blessing for Papa, too, because he was so alert to the end that had he remained conscious, it would have been sad for him to say goodbye to his Paolina.

News travels fast in the little town of Norway, Michigan – soon, relatives and friends came to the hospital, quietly keeping vigil in the corridor outside Papa's room.

In the first few minutes of October 6, 1991, Papa left his body and went home to heaven – to his beloved Jesus and Our Blessed Mother of Mount Carmel.

THE GOOD WORD

From the Pastor's Desk

It was certainly with a heavy heart that I announced on last Sunday morning the death of a man who had come to be known as Mr. St. Eulalia. It was also with a joyful spirit that I made that announcement; joyful because of the knowledge that the God that Joe Rauzi loved and served so faithfully all his life, he was now seeing face to face. Joe so loved his wife of 64 years, and his 7 children, and numerous grandchildren, and great-grandchildren, but he loved the Lord that much more, so much so that he lived out the Gospel directive to "die to himself, in order to live for others."

When I first arrived on the scene, over 8 years ago, I arrived during the summer months, a time that Joe and Pauline Rauzi typically spent in Norway, Michigan. All that summer, Monsignor Quinn kept telling me Joe Rauzi stories. Whenever I would ask about specific tasks that had to be done, Msgr. would generally say: "oh! don't worry about that Joe Rauzi does it." My reactions were, first, 'what am I going to do?' and secondly, 'can anyone be that efficient?' When the Rauzi's arrived in the Fall, I quickly found out just how efficient Joe was. He opened the church, turned on the heat, served every Mass, be it weekday, Sunday, wedding or funeral. At one time, Joe single-handedly did all the maintenance for the entire Parish plant, which also included the then little school. He drove the school bus, served on various committees and still found quality time to raise his family and become a man of deep spirituality. In the past several years when Joe's health began to deteriorate Joe could often be found either in Church praying before the Blessed Sacrament, or walking the streets with his rosary always in his hand. Joe's faith was private, but he lived it in very public ways. His devotion to priests and religious was at times very humbling. On many occasions Joe would simply take my hands to kiss them, or humbly ask for my blessing. Joe's love of the Eucharist, always indicated the recognition that this was his food for the journey, a journey that was graced with selfless love and giving. In Joe's simple but sublime faith, he understood the paradox of the Gospel, that if we pour out our lives in loving service, we shall gain an everlasting dwelling place in heaven. As Joe's pastor and as his friend I know that he's with the Lord in heaven, because of what heaven is. It's a place that opens its doors to lovers only, and Joe was a lover and a giver. Our parish and the church in general has been blessed with Joe's life, and the beauty of that is that we shall continue to be blessed with Joe's prayers and intercession from his heavenly reward.

Joe, you go before us into Galilee, and there we shall see you again.

CHAPTER 13

A LOVING FAREWELL

Precisely at the time of Papa's death, Sister Miriam saw a shadow cross her room, so when I called her, she already knew Papa was gone. Also at that same time, our son David was kneeling and praying for Grandpa. As he said it, "Mom, I don't know if I had fallen asleep and was dreaming or if I saw something, but I saw two big hands come out of the sky and scoop Grandpa up, taking him up to heaven. Grandpa looked real small in the hands, like a little child."

Also in those minutes, our son Joseph's friend, Lisa Belfiori, who was a very sensitive person, entered Joe's small Minneapolis apartment first. She immediately felt a presence there. Searching everywhere, she found no one. Then the phone call came announcing Papa's death. When Joe came into the apartment moments later, Lisa asked him to sit down and then told him about Papa. Joe said, as he demonstrated with his hands, "I felt a white light enter through the top of my head and go through my body, leaving my body through my feet. At that moment, before I said anything, Lisa said, 'He's gone.'" It would seem that Papa was saying a lot of goodbyes and in this instance, to his namesake.

The brothers arrived in Michigan and stayed with Mama, helping her as she greeted the many people who came to the house. They then closed up the cottage and helped Mama get ready to return to Maywood. One of the couples who came to the house that late night were Eddie and Bunnie Rizzi, the couple whose relationship Papa had encouraged thirty-five years earlier, who were also at their cottage in Michigan. Bunnie just climbed up onto the bed where Mama was resting and for an hour Bunnie hugged and comforted her.

After I made arrangements with the local funeral director to transport Papa back home to Maywood, I left for Green Bay, packed some things and left immediately for Illinois to prepare for the funeral. Deep down, I think I just needed to be home in Maywood, Papa's place. My husband and children came the next day. Sister Miriam, Uncle Bonnie and I had already made the funeral arrangements in advance, earlier that spring. Now, Father Quinlan helped prepare the church for Papa's wake, which was held in the church – the place he loved so much. Knowing Papa didn't want people to buy flowers, he brought beautiful potted green plants from other areas of the buildings and his two tall blooming hibiscus trees. Some people who didn't know Papa's wishes did send flowers and, appropriately for a man who loved them so much, Papa was surrounded by flowers and beautiful greenery.

The Knights of Columbus stood honor guard during the wake and funeral. Between Papa's nephews who are priests, the parish priests and deacons and former Saint Eulalia priests, there were eleven priests concelebrating the Mass, with Father Jim Quinlan as main celebrant, and Julio Camerini as deacon. It was estimated that over nine hundred or more people were present. The wake was in the afternoon with a seven o'clock Mass right after. Papa wanted this so that the working people could attend the Mass. The parish insisted on giving a reception in the church hall after the Mass. They graciously honored Papa one last time.

The following morning another Mass, which was supposed to be a private Mass, was celebrated by Father Gino Dalpiaz, Papa's nephew and godson, but again other priests returned.

Over three hundred people came back for this Mass and then to the cemetery. These were not just family members but many parishioners and friends as well.

As he wished, Papa's grave is a very simple one with just a small flat grave marker embedded in the ground, in the Sacred Heart of Jesus section of the cemetery. We laid him to rest in Queen of Heaven Cemetery, which is an extension of Mount Carmel Cemetery where Papa began his struggling, working, and happy years in America.

You have been told, O Man, what is good.
And what the Lord requires of you.
Only to do the right and to love goodness,
And to walk humbly with your God.

–Micah 6:8

EPILOGUE

MAMA

I stayed with Mama for three months after Papa died, as she grieved terribly. We went through the whole house at that time also, sorting, packing, giving away and throwing away. Even though Father Quinlan told Mama that she could stay in the house as long as she wanted, Mama would not stay in her home alone. She had never slept in a house alone in her entire life.

Her Joe was gone and now she was relinquishing the things of her homemaking, being a wife and mother, all her identity as she knew it. This was a terrible time in her life. Blessedly some of the furnishings and favorite things went with her to the convent and some to the Michigan house. Finally she moved to the convent motherhouse to live with our sister, Sister Miriam Dolores. After she moved out of the house, Father Quinlan had a plaque made and secured it to the back of the house where parishioners could readily see it. It simply reads, RAUZI HOUSE.

Rauzi House -- our home.

For seven years Mama lived happily at the convent and was wonderfully, lovingly taken care of by Sister Miriam. She had a suite of rooms; a bedroom, livingroom and bathroom. She also had great friendships with the Sisters and she wasn't forgotten by family and friends who came often to visit.

Sister Miriam and I, the boys and their wives, took turns staying with Mama in Michigan for a couple of months each summer until Mama's confusion and loss of memory became very apparent. While Sister Miriam and Mama were in Michigan in 1998, Sister Miriam had to be hospitalized with a diabetic problem and Mama came home with me to Green Bay to live. By this time, she needed someone to watch over her at all times. Part of Mama's illness was falling. No matter what we did to protect her, she fell more and more frequently. The doctor insisted she be placed in a twenty-four-hour care facility where I visited her daily. Four months later, she fell and broke her hip. From that point on, she went from being a talkative and very sociable woman to a quiet lady who was slipping away.

The entire family came to Green Bay for her ninety-first birthday. Weeks later, on April 17, 1999, she went to heaven to be with her loving Lord and "her Joe." Mama's wake and funeral were held at our sister's convent motherhouse in LaGrange Park, Illinois.